EDGAR ALLAN POE

EDGAR ALLAN POE

MASTER OF SUSPENSE

TRISTAN BOYER BINNS

FRANKLIN WATTS
A Division of Scholastic Inc.
New York Toronto London Auckland Sydney
Mexico City New Delhi Hong Kong
Danbury, Connecticut

For my father, Jon Frederick Boyer, an interesting character himself

ACKNOWLEDGMENTS

The author would like to thank the following for permission to reproduce material:

Letters from John Allan to Charles Ellis in Chapter One, letter from John Allan to William Henry Poe in Chapter Two, letter from John Allan to his sister in Chapter Three, from the Ellis & Allan Company Records, Manuscript Division, Library of Congress.

Letters from Elmira Royster Shelton and Miles George to Edward V. Valentine in Chapter Two, letters from Poe to John Allan in Chapters Three, Four, and Five, letter from John Allan to Major John Eaton in Chapter Four, letter from Poe to Sergeant Graves in Chapter Four, from the Valentine Richmond History Center.

Letter from Poe to Thomas W. White in Chapter Five, letter from Poe to Thomas Chivers in Chapter Nine, from the Huntington Library, San Marino, California.

Letters from Poe to John Pendleton Kennedy in Chapter Six, from the Papers of John Pendleton Kennedy, Archives of the Peabody Institute of the Johns Hopkins University.

Letter from Thomas W. White to Poe in Chapter Six, letter from Poe to Frederick Thomas in Chapter Nine, letter form Poe to F. W. Thomas in Chapter Ten, from the Boston Public Library/Rare Books Department. Courtesy of the Trustees.

Letters from Poe to George Eveleth in Chapter Ten, from the Pierpont Morgan Library, New York.

Photographs are copyrighted by their original source and all rights are reserved. Copyright and credits for individual photographs can be found on page 128.

Library of Congress Cataloging-in-Publication Data

Binns, Tristan Boyer, 1968–
   Edgar Allan Poe : master of suspense / Tristan Boyer Binns.
      p. cm. — (Great life stories)
   Includes bibliographical references (p.   ) and index.
   ISBN 0-531-16751-8 (alk. paper)
   1. Poe, Edgar Allan, 1809–1849—Juvenile literature. 2. Authors, American—19th century—Biography—Juvenile literature. 3. Suspense fiction—Authorship—Juvenile literature. I. Title. II. Series.
   PS2631.B48 2005
   818'.309—dc22   2005011163

Printed in the United States of America.
1 2 3 4 5 6 7 8 9 10 R 14 13 12 11 10 09 08 07 06 05

CONTENTS

It is likely that Poe's parents took their infant son to Baltimore (shown here) in 1809.

A Hard Beginning

On January 19, 1809, Elizabeth Poe gave birth to her second child, a boy named Edgar. He was to become a great and inventive writer and lead a puzzling, difficult life. Elizabeth and her husband, David Poe Jr., already had a son, born two years earlier, named William Henry Leonard. Elizabeth and David were actors and had little money. They spent their lives traveling between theaters and performing a wide range of roles. They were popular performers in Boston, where Edgar was born. Three weeks after his birth, Elizabeth was back on the stage.

When Edgar was born, David had to beg for money from his family to keep them going. It was hard for them to look after babies and work most evenings as well. Elizabeth and David may have taken Edgar to stay with David's parents in Baltimore when he was about one month old.

He was collected again about six months later. The Poe grandparents probably looked after William Henry at times as well.

David's father, General David Poe, was a hero of the Revolutionary War. He and his wife were both of Irish descent. They lived in Baltimore. David Jr. was born in 1784 in Baltimore.

Elizabeth was born in England in about 1787. She sailed for the United States with her mother when she was nine. Her mother was also an actor, and Elizabeth first performed in the United States soon after they arrived. Elizabeth's mother died when she was eleven years old. Elizabeth married in 1802, but her husband died in 1805. David Poe began acting with her in 1804 and, in 1806, David and Elizabeth married. Elizabeth was well-known, and according to the critics who reviewed theater at that time, a very talented actor. David faced more criticism and was probably not as good an actor as his wife, but he received many fine reviews as well.

In September 1809, Elizabeth and David Poe were playing at the Park Theatre in New York. David Poe made his last known appearance on October 18. After that no one knows what happened to him. He was probably in New York with his family, perhaps ill. Elizabeth stayed in New York until July 1810. She then moved on to Richmond, Virginia. Her third child, Rosalie, was born in Norfolk, probably on December 20, 1810. In January 1811, Elizabeth was back on the stage in

Today, New York City's theater district is commonly known as "Broadway." But in the early 1800s, a different kind of stage ruled the famous avenue—stagecoaches!

THEATER IN EARLY AMERICA

In the early 1800s, theaters were important gathering places. Before movies and television, they were one of the main forms of entertainment in towns and cities. Sometimes theaters closed because epidemics of illness swept through a city. Some theaters had seasons, and closed out of season. Actors had to move a lot to keep working. If the didn't, they couldn't earn enough money to support themselves. They also had to know many roles. They performed opera, Shakespeare, comedies, and dramas. Theaters changed the plays they produced often. Each day's playbill usually included two or more plays and songs as well.

Charleston, South Carolina. In June, she moved on to Norfolk. No one is sure when or where David Poe died, but there is no record of his being with his wife and children after the end of July 1811. It is assumed that he died sometime before then.

Elizabeth Poe became ill and gave her last performance on October 11, 1811. There were benefit performances at the theater to raise money for her. Public notices in newspapers stated how ill she was and asked people to help her. Her fans brought nurses and cooks and tried to make her comfortable. She died on December 8 with her children at her side. William Henry said she spoke a "long . . . last farewell" to them. Edgar was almost three. Elizabeth left him a painting she made of Boston Harbor, a miniature painting of herself, and some letters. Edgar's life of traveling between theaters, with its poverty and excitement, was over.

A NEW FAMILY

Soon after his mother's death, a local businessman and his wife took in Edgar. John and Frances Allan had no children of their own. Frances was charmed by Edgar and convinced John to give him a home. William Henry was cared for by his grandparents in Baltimore, and Rosalie was taken in by William and Jane Mackenzie, neighbors of the Allans in Richmond.

John Allan was born in Scotland and came to the United States to work for his rich uncle, William Galt. He had struggled through a hard apprenticeship but was doing well for himself. Allan was a shrewd businessman and could be very stern and demanding. He also had a lively sense of humor and wrote interesting, playful letters. Frances had been an orphan herself. She was often ill. She was not very well educated, but had a good sense of fun.

RICHMOND IN 1811

By 1811, Virginia's capital was a quickly growing town. Tobacco plantations flourished, making planters and business owners rich. Coal mines and flour mills along the James River added to Richmond's wealth. About six thousand free people and four thousand slaves were living there. A period of rapid building had just begun. Roads and sidewalks were being paved. New houses were going up, most two stories tall. Most of the buildings looked classical, were square in shape, and had columns at the fronts and backs. Thomas Jefferson designed the capitol, which stood in the center of town. His design was based on a Roman temple in France.

Frances's sister Nancy lived with the Allans. Their home was above the store that John Allan ran with his business partner, Charles Ellis. They had money because the business was doing well. They sold all kinds of merchandise to local people, as general stores of the day did. They also sold tobacco and flour to people in other countries.

John and Frances Allan liked to enjoy themselves. They were part of the social scene in Richmond and entertained at their home as well. They played cards and went to the theater.

Edgar was treated like a son, but the Allans never adopted him. John Allan had a crib made for him and bought him clothes. Edgar traveled with the family when they traveled to a resort called White Sulphur Springs, where wealthy people went to escape Richmond's summer heat.

In 1813, Edgar had whooping cough and measles but recovered. It's likely that he saw his sister, Rosalie, from time to time. He didn't see William Henry, who stayed in Baltimore. When Edgar was five, he went to his first teacher, Clotilda Fisher. Later, he was taught by William Ewing. He lived at home during these school years.

LIVING IN LONDON

In June 1815, the Allans went to London to expand their business. Frances and Nancy were very sick during the trip across the Atlantic Ocean. Frances never really recovered her health and spent a great deal of her time in England trying to get well again. She was homesick, too. They all went to Scotland to see John Allan's family then settled in London.

At first, life was pleasant in London. There were sights to see and a huge new city to explore. Allan wrote to Charles Ellis that one night

they were "by a snug fire in a nice little sitting parlour in [our home] with Frances and Nancy Sewing and Edgar reading a little Story Book." Edgar was known as Edgar Allan instead of Edgar Poe. He called Allan "Pa." When Edgar was seven, he went to a boarding school run by the Dubourg sisters. He was only about 3 miles (4.8 kilometers) away from the Allan home in London. While they were in England, Edgar's grandfather, General David Poe, died in Baltimore.

At the age of nine, Edgar went to the Manor House School in Stoke Newington. It was a better and more expensive school in the country near London. There Edgar learned French, Latin, history, and literature. His teacher said he did well and was a "quick and clever boy." He also said Edgar was "intelligent, wayward, and wilful." Allan paid his bills and encouraged his work. In 1818, he wrote to Charles Ellis, "Edgar is growing wonderfully and enjoys a good reputation as both able and willing to receive instruction."

Days were long at Manor House School, and the work was hard. Students had very little freedom and were watched carefully by their teachers. Edgar used the Manor House School as the setting for one of his stories, "William Wilson," published in 1838. In this story he wrote:

> My earliest recollections of school-life are connected with a large, rambling, cottage-built, and somewhat decayed building in a misty-looking village of England, where were a vast number of gigantic and gnarled trees, and where all the houses were excessively ancient and inordinately tall. In truth, it was a dream-like and spirit-soothing place, that venerable old town.

There isn't a lot of information about Edgar during this time, but he was probably lonely. He may have gone home for the weekends. With Frances weak and Allan busy trying to make money, life at home couldn't have been much fun. Frances seldom wrote. There are no letters from her to Edgar, and she doesn't mention him in the few letters she wrote to her husband. John Allan often mentioned Edgar in his letters, but as his business grew worse, he started leaving Edgar out of them.

The business in England was not a success. The country's economy was weak and ultimately crashed. Allan went from making money to owing a lot of it. His creditors gave him a year to pay off his debts. In March 1820, Allan wrote to Charles Ellis, "The truth is Charles we have erred through pride and ambition. I hope we shall yet have an opportunity to conduct our business like sensible and reflecting men." He wanted to go home. In July 1820, the Allans sailed for the United States. Frances was very sick again during the voyage. The family arrived safely back in Richmond on August 2.

Richmond, Virginia, was a unique American city in the early 1800s. It was set between the North and the South. It was more industrial than most Southern cities but relied on slave labor. Most Northern cities didn't use slave labor.

EDGAR AND ALLAN

When the Allans returned to Richmond, they moved into Charles Ellis's house. They lived there for about a year and then moved into a house of their own. Allan and Ellis worked hard to rebuild their business, but it was a struggle.

Back in the United States, Edgar was known as Edgar Poe again, not Edgar Allan. Some of his friends say he was a leader. Others say that even though he was a good student and likeable, he was never really accepted because he was a foster child and the son of actors. Richmond had a class-based society. The planters were at the top, and the merchants and businessmen were in the middle. As the foster son of a businessman, Edgar had less social standing than he would have liked. All his life he showed charm and great manners and dressed well. He had a quick wit

Traveling Around

In the early 1800s, people traveled mainly on foot, by horse, or by boat. Most cities were very small. People could walk from one side to the other in less than a half-hour. People rode their own horses or drove their own carriages as well. In the city, the first horse-drawn buses could carry about twelve passengers. To travel farther on land, people rode on horse-drawn stagecoaches that were bumpy and uncomfortable. Most cities were located on rivers or oceans with busy ports. Traveling by boat was usually quicker and more comfortable. The only way to get to Europe was by boat. The trip usually took five weeks.

and a gift for language. He tried to fit in with his social betters and usually succeeded.

Edgar lived at home and went to a nearby school run by Joseph Clarke. He learned Latin and Greek and probably studied English and math as well. His teacher said he was enthusiastic, self-respecting, and stubborn. He had great imagination and "a sensitive and tender heart." He spoke and read poetry well and won prizes for it. His teacher also said, "Poe wrote genuine poetry: The boy was a born poet."

Meanwhile, John Allan was busy with his business. But he was aware of Edgar's writing skills and was proud of the boy. He even showed Joseph Clarke some of Edgar's poems. Allan wanted to know if he should publish Edgar's poems, but Clarke said it would just make Edgar vain.

In 1822, the Allans moved again. In 1823, Edgar began attending William Burke's school, where he became known for his abilities in

Latin and French. He was also in very good physical shape. He famously swam 6 miles (9.7 km) against the tide in the James River. He boxed and ran on school teams. His new friends and teachers were also impressed by his poetry.

The earliest-known poem composed by Edgar comes from 1824. It was written on a paper that had sums showing how much money the Allans' business had stored for an emergency. It was in the files at Ellis & Allan. The poem reads:

—Poetry. by . Edgar A. Poe—
Last night with many cares & toils oppress'd
Weary, I laid me on a couch to rest—

This poem, written by Poe at age nineteen, displays his distinctive handwriting.

Frances Allan (above) was Poe's foster mother, but he "adopted" other mother figures throughout his life.

At the age of fifteen, Edgar became a lieutenant in the Junior Morgan Riflemen. This group of volunteers paraded in front of famous military visitors and practiced drills. Edgar enjoyed the military work. It reminded him of his famous grandfather, General David Poe.

TROUBLES AT HOME

One of Edgar's schoolmates once wrote, "It was a noticeable fact that he never asked any of his schoolmates to go home with him after school. Other boys would frequently spend the night or take dinner with each other at their homes. . . ." One of Edgar's few friends at school was Robert Stanard. Robert's mother, Jane, was a kind and beautiful woman. Edgar was about fourteen years old when he met her. He came to think of her as a substitute mother. Frances Allan was seldom well. Even though Edgar and Frances clearly were very fond of each other, Edgar may have felt he needed a more sympathetic "mother." In April 1824, Jane Stanard died after a period of mental illness. Edgar was very upset and took to visiting her grave at night.

After Jane Stanard died, Edgar grew more unhappy. He was probably feeling lonely and was unsure of his standing with the Allans and in society. Soon after her death, John Allan wrote a letter about Edgar to Edgar's brother William Henry, now known simply as Henry. "He . . . seems quite miserable, sulky & ill-tempered to all the Family. How we have acted to produce this is beyond my conception—why I have put up so long with his conduct is little less wonderful. The boy possesses not a Spark of affection for us not a particle of gratitude for all my care and kindness towards him."

John Allan was still facing business troubles and probably felt worried and tense himself. In December 1824, John Allan and Charles Ellis ended their partnership. Allan's uncle William Galt helped bail him out of his financial difficulties. From this point on, Allan's relationship with Edgar grew strained. Allan had been having affairs during his marriage and had at least one illegitimate child. Edgar may have known about Allan's affairs and could have been angry about them. Even if Frances wasn't the most engaged foster mother, she was still the closest thing he had to one. It's likely that Edgar would have been upset that Allan dishonored Frances by having affairs.

In 1825, Henry probably visited Edgar. Edgar also saw his sister, Rosalie, from time to time. Rosalie was not a very strong or healthy girl and may have had learning difficulties.

In March 1825, William Galt died, leaving his fortune to John Allan. Suddenly John and Frances were well off, bought a mansion, and entertained as they liked to. Allan was a thrifty man, even when he became rich. His habit of writing down all the money spent by his household in great detail never left him. He even wrote down the few pennies paid for postage on letters.

Edgar moved into the new mansion. He enjoyed meeting the important people of Richmond who came to call. Edgar now felt himself to be part of the upper class.

Edgar met Elmira Royster when he was about sixteen years old. The two fell in love. Elmira later told a writer about Edgar, "He was a beautiful boy—Not very talkative. When he did talk though he was pleasant but his general manner was sad . . . He had strong prejudices. Hated anything coarse and unrefined. . . . He was as warm and zealous in any cause he was interested in, very enthusiastic and impulsive. . . ." Elmira and Edgar were engaged, but her father thought she was too

Living in the Allan mansion, Poe may have felt more comfortable about his status in Richmond society.

THE UNIVERSITY OF VIRGINIA

Thomas Jefferson founded the University of Virginia in Charlottesville to teach students in complete educational freedom. This meant students would be able to choose what they studied and that the college would have no official religion. The students were responsible for making and enforcing the rules. There was no president. At the time, it was the most expensive college in the United States. Most students were wealthy. They kept slaves or servants and lived well. Most drank and gambled. College life was full of fights, riots, and violence. After a short time the faculty demanded that the students be given a set of rules to follow.

young to marry. He also may have been worried that Edgar was an orphan, too young, and had no profession.

POE ATTENDS UNIVERSITY

In February 1826, at just seventeen years old, Edgar went to the University of Virginia. It had only been open a year. When Edgar arrived, the rotunda, a large round room, was still being built, and the library was not yet opened. Edgar A. Poe signed on to study ancient and modern languages.

There were only two hours of class per day, six days a week. The students had a lot of studying to do but also had a lot of free time. Edgar joined the debating club and did well. Some of the other students remembered Edgar as a good student, especially in modern languages.

One fellow student later wrote about Edgar, "He was very excitable & restless, at times wayward, melancholic & morose, but again in his better moods frolicksome, full of fun & a most attractive & agreeable companion[.] To calm & quiet the excessive nervous excitability under which he labored, he would too often put himself under the influence of [wine]." Another said, "Poe's passion for strong drink was as marked and as peculiar as that for cards." Edgar had started drinking and gambling.

Accounts vary about Edgar and his lifelong problem with alcohol. Some people said he drank heavily for long stretches. Others said that after one drink, he would be unable to carry on. It seems that alcohol affected Edgar greatly. He was usually very sick for days after drinking. Some people think he had a disease such as diabetes, which meant his body couldn't handle alcohol, so even a little bit would make him ill. Whatever the truth was, Edgar would have binges and "dry" stretches for the rest of his life.

From the beginning, Allan didn't give Edgar enough money to cover his expenses. Without a proper budget, Edgar was on his own for the first time. A series of letters began between the two men at about this time. Edgar told Allan the news, especially about the violent fights around him. He explained how he was short of money and begged for more. Allan wrote back accusing Edgar of living too well, but he sent some of the money Edgar needed.

Allan also sent Edgar books and clothes. He seems to have been unwilling to cut Edgar off but also unwilling to take care of him completely. Edgar made the excuse that he took up gambling to try to pay off his debts. He wanted to live like his fellow students. Betting on card games and dressing well were examples of normal behavior. Edgar borrowed money at high rates of interest and left IOUs and debts in his wake.

In December 1826, Edgar took exams. He is listed as having excelled at ancient languages and French. On December 21, he left for Richmond. His debts were somewhere between $2,000 and $2,500, a huge amount of money at the time. One account says that Allan went to Charlottesville, paid "every debt that he thought ought to be paid," but refused to pay Edgar's gambling debts. Others say that Edgar was hounded by his creditors and faced going to prison for his debts.

When he got home, Edgar was confronted with two bitter disappointments. He found out that all the letters he had written to Elmira Royster had been kept, unopened, by her father. She was engaged to another man. Edgar must have been very upset, but there isn't any firsthand account of how he felt. Also, though many students only went to the university for a term or a year, Edgar wanted to return and keep studying. Unfortunately, John Allan refused to send him back for another term.

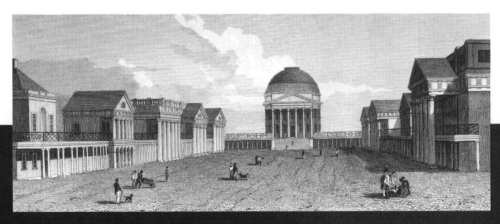

Thomas Jefferson designed the buildings, as well as the academic program, at the University of Virginia.

In Poe's time, people who owed debts and couldn't pay were sometimes imprisoned. Poe hoped Allan would save him from this fate.

THREE

THE ARMY
AND POETRY

No one is sure what Edgar Allan Poe did from January to March 1827 after moving back to Richmond. Some say he worked for Ellis & Allan, others that he started to study law. We know that by March he was in trouble. The people he owed money to were trying to have him arrested. Poe had turned eighteen years old in January and was now old enough to go to prison for owing money. John Allan refused to pay his debts.

Poe and Allan had an argument. On March 19, 1827, Poe wrote to Allan:

. . . you have blasted my hope [to go back to the University of Virginia]. . . . Again, I have heard you say (when you little thought I was listening and therefore must have said it in earnest) that you had no affection for me—You have moreover ordered me to quit your house. . . . and I am gone—

Poe accused Allan of spoiling his chances of getting an education and a good career. He also said that Allan was letting all the servants in the household treat him badly.

Poe left home and took a room at a tavern nearby. Frances probably wrote Poe two letters that March. On March 20, Poe wrote to Allan again. He asked for "the expense of my passage to Boston ($12) and a little to support me there until I shall be enabled to engage in some

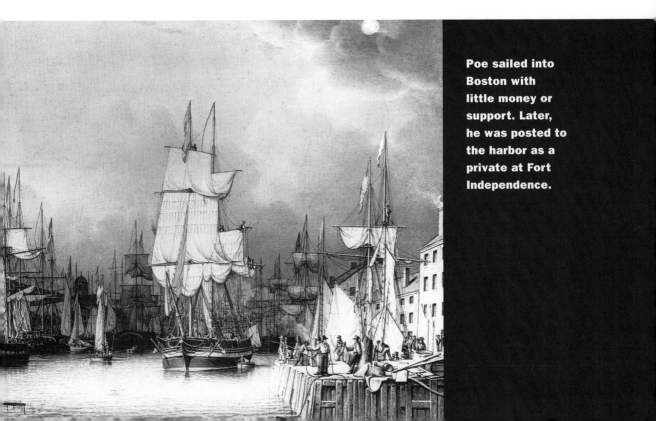

Poe sailed into Boston with little money or support. Later, he was posted to the harbor as a private at Fort Independence.

business. I sail on Saturday. . . . I have not one cent to provide any food." Allan wrote back, saying that Poe had not been working hard enough. It appears that he sent no money.

Perhaps Poe borrowed the money he needed from a friend. He sailed for Boston, probably on Saturday, March 24, 1827. He may have stopped in Baltimore on the way to see his brother, Henry. On March 27, Allan wrote to his sister, "I'm thinking Edgar has gone to Sea to seek his own fortunes." During the rest of the spring, Allan kept getting letters from Poe's creditors asking him to pay debts Poe ran up while at the university.

Poe was in Boston in April. No one knows what he did until the end of May. He may have worked as a clerk or as an actor. He was surely writing poetry and didn't have much money. There are wild stories that he went to fight in Greece, then on to Saint Petersburg, Russia. The truth is that on May 26, 1827, he signed on as a private in the U.S. Army.

Poe gave a false name and age when he joined the army. He said he was Edgar A. Perry, age twenty-two. He agreed to stay in the army for five years. He was posted to Fort Independence, Boston Harbor. Life in the army suited Poe. He had the ability to do well and wanted to succeed.

HIS FIRST BOOK

In the summer after he joined the army, Poe's first book was published. It was called *Tamerlane, and Other Poems*. Poe is not named as the author. The book says it is "by a Bostonian." It was listed but not reviewed in the literary magazines of the day. Fifty copies were printed, but there is no evidence that they sold. Poe was one of the first literary greats of the United States, but it was a number of years before anyone recognized this.

AMERICAN WRITING

When the United States was founded, most literature came from England and the rest of Europe. By the 1820s, Americans were starting to create their own literature. Reading and discussing new writing was a popular pastime. Some American books were published, but magazines were more popular. Most writers at the time published stories, poems, essays, and reviews in magazines. The majority of writing was reviewed in literary magazines.

Poe claimed that all the poems in his first book were written before he was fourteen. This was probably an exaggeration. Because Poe was only eighteen, they were clearly written when he was young. He wrote about beauty, love, pride, and death. He showed an early ability with words and meter. As Poe developed his skills as a poet, he got better and better at using words. He believed the meaning of the words was not all that mattered. How they sounded when spoken was just as important. They had to rhyme in the right places. The syllables had to have the right stresses. Read out loud, this part of "Tamerlane" shows Poe's attention to how the words sound:

Among the rabble-men
Lion ambition is chain'd down
And crouches to a keeper's hand—
Not so in deserts where the grand
The wild—the terrible conspire
With their own breath to fan his fire.

Poe always reworked his poetry. Even after it had been published, he kept revising it. For example, "Tamerlane" went through at least five revisions between 1827 and 1845. It varied between 406 and 234 lines in length.

At the same time, Edgar's brother, Henry, was also writing. He was not as good a writer as Edgar but had enough talent to get published. Henry was working on the USS *Macedonian,* sailing to South America, when his first poem came out in the *Saturday Evening Post.* Some of Edgar's work was published under Henry's name in the magazine the *North American.* Henry also published a number of poems and stories in the *North American* before it folded at the end of 1828.

At the end of October 1827, Edgar Allan Poe's battery was ordered to move to Fort Moultrie on Sullivan's Island in Charleston, South Carolina. They had a stormy trip by boat. Poe probably visited people in Charleston

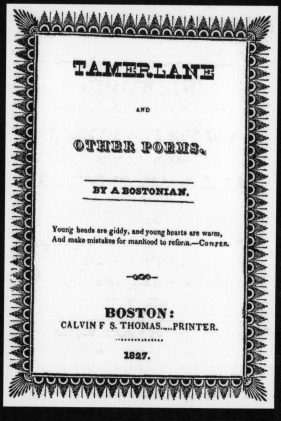

Tamerlane, and Other Poems was published in 1827, but Poe revised the title poem throughout his life.

and joined in society gatherings as much as possible. Later, he used Sullivan's Island as the setting for his story, "The Gold-Bug."

ASKING FOR HELP

At the end of October 1828, Poe's military unit was ordered to Fortress Monroe at Old Point Comfort, Virginia. Before they went, Poe decided he had had enough of the army. Poe asked Lieutenant Howard, one of his officers, to write to John Allan. Howard agreed to let Poe leave the army if Allan and Poe made up. Allan wrote back to Howard, saying, "He had better remain as he is until the termination of his enlistment." Poe

Poe spent a year posted at Fort Moultrie, on Sullivan's Island. In his story "The Gold-Bug," three men search for buried treasure on the island.

then wrote to John Allan, probably for the first time since he had left Richmond. Poe was concerned because he heard that Allan had been ill. He went on to talk about leaving the army.

It was perhaps under the impression that a military life was one after my own heart . . . but I could not help thinking that you believed me degraded & disgraced and that any thing were preferable to my returning home. . . . But at no period of my life have I regarded myself with a deeper satisfaction—or did my heart swell with more honourable pride . . .

I have been in the American army as long as suits my ends or my inclination, and it is now time that I should leave it . . .

The period of Enlistment is five years—the prime of my life would be wasted—I shall be driven to more decided measures if you refuse to assist me. You need not fear for my future prosperity—I am altered from what you knew me. . . . I have thrown myself on the world . . . I must either conquer or die—succeed or be disgraced. . . .

Write me once more if you really do forgive me, let me know how my Ma preserves her health, and the concerns of the family since my departure. . . . My dearest love to Ma—it is only when absent that we can tell the value of such a friend—I hope she will not let my wayward disposition wear away the love she used to have for me.

Allan didn't write back to this pleading and at times threatening letter. Poe wrote again three weeks later, after the battery had moved. It was December 22, 1828.

[It upsets me that] you who called me your son should refuse me even the common civility of answering a letter. If it is your wish to forget that I have been your son I am too proud to remind you of it again. . . .

My father do not throw me aside . . . I will be an honor to your name.

Give my best love to Ma & to all friends—If you determine to abandon me—here take our farewell—Neglected—I will be doubly ambitious, & the world shall hear of the son whom you have thought unworthy of your notice. But if you let the love you bear me outweigh the offence which I have given—then write me my father, quickly.

Poe was asking for Allan's help, pleading to be recognized again. He clearly didn't mean that he would actually go away if Allan refused to write back or help him. Poe's letters appear disorganized. He doesn't seem to be sure of his status. Was he like a real son, who always has a connection to his family? Or had he truly been cut off without any future hopes? Allan must have been puzzled as well. After not hearing from Poe for twenty-one months, his sudden demands for help must have been a surprise. Allan may have thought Poe only wanted him for money or career help, to bail him out when he was in trouble. Poe's creditors were still chasing Allan for payment of Poe's debts. Allan never wrote back to Poe.

On January 1, 1829, Poe was promoted to sergeant major. He couldn't reach a higher rank without going to the U.S. Military Academy at West Point and studying to become an officer. On February 4, Poe wrote again to Allan. He wanted Allan to use his influence to get him a place at West Point. Poe claimed he would speed through in six months. He also said he needed money again. He tried to apologize for his debts and bad behavior at the university but also excused himself at the same time. "I had never been away from home before for any length of time. I say again I have no excuse to offer for my conduct except that common one of youth." At the end of the letter, he threatened to leave the United States if Allan didn't help him. Once again, Allan didn't reply.

On February 28, 1829, Frances Allan died. Poe didn't make it back to Richmond until the day after she was buried. No one knows if Frances asked John to help Poe before she died, but somehow Allan and Poe made up. Allan bought Poe new clothes. He agreed to get Poe out of the army and help get him into West Point.

In this December 1, 1828, letter to John Allan, Poe tries to assert his confidence and newfound independence.

West Point, on the western bank of the Hudson River, is the site of the U.S. Military Academy. It was established by Congress in 1802.

FOUR

FROM WEST POINT TO POVERTY

Edgar Allan Poe returned to Fortress Monroe. He wrote to John Allan on March 10, calling him "My dear Pa." He explained how happy he felt that they had made up and how sad he was about Frances's death. By the end of March, his commander had written to his superior to ask for Poe's discharge. On April 15, 1829, Poe was officially discharged. He had to pay a substitute to take his place. The man he found was Sergeant Samuel Graves. Usually the fee for a substitute was twelve dollars. For some reason, this wasn't the case for Poe. He had to pay Sergeant Graves seventy-five dollars, but he only had twenty-five dollars to give him. Poe gave Graves an IOU for the rest. Poe didn't tell Allan about the extra cost.

Maria Clemm became one of the most important people in Poe's life. Though twenty years older than Poe, she lived more than twenty years longer than he did.

Next Poe had to secure a place at West Point. He needed to apply to the secretary of war in Washington, D.C. Three of Poe's officers wrote letters of recommendation. They said he did his work well, didn't drink, was faithful, and deserved confidence. Poe took the letters home to Richmond. There two of John Allan's friends also wrote letters for Poe. One was the speaker of the House of Representatives, who "most earnestly" recommended Poe. Allan himself wrote an odd letter, saying Poe had left him because of his gambling debts. Allan said Poe was a good student and the grandson of General David Poe. Then he said:

> Frankly Sir, do I declare that He is no relation to me whatever; that I have many [in] whom I have taken an active Interest to promote theirs; with no other feeling than that, every Man is my care, if he be in distress; for myself I ask nothing but I do request your kindness to aid this youth in the promotion of his future prospects.

Poe took his letters to Washington, D.C., early in May. Allan gave him fifty dollars for his trip. Poe collected more recommendations and presented them to the secretary of war. He hoped to get a place at West Point the following September. Then Poe went to see his family in Baltimore.

IN BALTIMORE

Poe's grandmother was suffering from paralysis. She lived with her widowed daughter, Poe's aunt, Maria Clemm. Maria had two children, Henry and Virginia, then ages eleven and six. Poe's brother, Henry, also lived with them in their small house. They had General Poe's pension to live on, but little else. Maria kept the family going. Henry Poe was "entirely given up to drink & unable to help himself." He still published his work but had given up his career in the navy. Edgar visited and got more involved with the family as time went on. Maria helped by sewing some clothes for him. Other cousins lived nearby, and Poe was also in contact with them.

Baltimore experienced a period of growth after organizing the construction of America's first railroad in 1828.

BALTIMORE IN THE EARLY 1800S

Poe found the busy seaport of Baltimore more exciting than Richmond. With a population of about eighty thousand, it was the third-largest city in the United States. The port was home to two steamboat lines. There were busy markets and hotels and good food. People lived in brick houses facing wide streets. Almost everyone could see the 160-foot (48.8-meter) tall marble column topped with a statue of George Washington. Baltimore's Catholic church had the largest pipe organ in the United States. In 1830, the first American passengers to ride in a steam-driven train did so in Baltimore.

Poe kept writing to Allan, who grew more short-tempered with him. Poe asked for money in almost every letter. By the end of the summer, Allan told Poe he was not wanted back in Richmond. Allan sent Poe enough money to live on modestly but made Poe beg for it. By Poe's account, he was living badly, with tattered clothes and constant worries about money. He lived in boardinghouses because "Grandmother is not in a situation to give me any accommodation." He was even robbed by his cousin. He was waiting for his West Point place to come through and wasn't sure when it would. At the end of July, Poe walked to Washington, D.C., and back. He was told there were ten names on the list ahead of him, and he would get into West Point by the following June at the latest.

Poe had been writing poetry while in the army. He tried to get his latest work, "Al Aaraaf," published as soon as he reached Baltimore. He asked for a recommendation from William Wirt, a writer, lawyer, and politician. Wirt told him to take it to Robert Walsh, editor of *American*

Quarterly Review in Philadelphia. Poe went off to Philadelphia and was told how hard it was to get a poem published. He kept trying back in Baltimore. The *Federal Gazette and Baltimore Daily Advertiser* published some of it on May 18. Poe submitted it to the publishers Carey, Lea & Carey. In the letter he sent with the manuscript, he said, "If the poem is published, succeed or not, I am 'irrecoverably a poet.'" Poe asked Allan to guarantee the one hundred dollars he thought it would cost to publish "Al Aaraaf" as a book. Allan refused.

Poe eventually found a different publisher for his book, Hatch & Dunning. *Al Aaraaf, Tamerlane, and Minor Poems* came out in December 1829. It received some good reviews. John Neal, of the *The Yankee and Boston Literary Gazette,* liked Poe's work. He said, "If the young author now before us should fulfil his destiny . . . he will be *foremost* in the rank of *real* poets." Most Poe critics think "Al

William Wirt advised Poe to publish "Al Aaraaf" in the *American Quarterly Review.* A few years later, Wirt ran unsuccessfully for president.

West Point

In 1802, the military post of West Point became a school to train officers for the U.S. Army. It sits about 50 miles (80.5 km) north of New York City, on the Hudson River. New students, called cadets, took an entrance exam to prove they could read, write, and do math. Their studies included French, math, drills, shooting, and guard duty. Their tightly scheduled days started at 5 A.M. Cadets had to know and follow 304 regulations. By 1830, about 130 cadets started each year. At the end of the four-year course, only about one-third graduated.

Aaraaf" is not one of his best works. It uses imagination but doesn't show Poe's spark and gift with words.

It is believed that Poe was welcomed home to Richmond again in January 1830. Despite their disagreements, Allan ultimately bought Poe new clothes. At the end of March, Poe was officially given a place at West Point, to start in June. At the end of May, Poe left for West Point.

WEST POINT

Poe broke up his journey to West Point with a stop in Baltimore. He arrived at West Point about June 20, 1830. After the entrance exam was over, Poe started summer military training with his fellow cadets. In September, they started academic work. Poe did well, having had plenty of experience with military and academic work before. He wrote Allan on November 6, "I have a very excellent standing in my class—in the first section in every thing and have great hopes of doing well."

Poe's friends were mostly from Virginia. They described him as careworn and reserved. He also seems to have broken the rule prohibiting drinking by sneaking out after hours to buy liquor. One student wrote, "He is thought a fellow of talent here but he is too mad a poet to like Mathematics."

John Allan had been having an affair with a woman named Elizabeth Wills. In July 1830, she had twin boys. Allan recognized them in his will as his sons. Then Allan went on to marry Louisa Patterson. She was from a good family in New Jersey. They wed on October 5, 1830, in New York. Poe wasn't invited to the wedding, and Allan didn't visit Poe when he was in New York.

At West Point, cadets are responsible for military drills, including weapons practice.

Poe was sent to West Point without enough money to cover his expenses. He started off in debt as he had done at the University of Virginia. In the spring of 1830, Sergeant Graves began asking for the fifty dollars Poe owed him. Poe wrote back, saying, "Mr A[llan] is not very often sober. . . . I have tried to get the money for you from Mr A a dozen times." Both of these things were probably not true. In January 1831, Allan found out about the accusations. He wrote to Poe for the last time, telling him their relationship was over. On January 3, Poe wrote back a long and nasty letter, full of accusations and excuses.

Did I, when an infant, [ask] your charity and protection, or was it of your own free will . . . ? . . . Under such circumstances, can it be said that I have no right to expect anything at your hands? . . . Your love I never valued—but she [Frances] I believe loved me as her own child. You promised me to forgive all—but you soon forgot your promise. You sent me to W. Point like a beggar. The same diffi-culties are threatening me as before at Charlottesville—and I must resign. . . . I have no energy left, nor health.

Allan never wrote back. He wrote in his notes, "I do not think the Boy has one good quality. He may do or act as he pleases."

After this, Poe simply stopped going to classes and drills. One of his friends later wrote, "It was only a few weeks after the beginning of his career at West Point that he seemed to lose interest in his studies and to be disheartened and discouraged." Poe was charged with gross neglect of duty on January 28. He was dismissed.

Poe left West Point on February 19. He had found a publisher in

New York, Elam Bliss, to put out his third book of poems. Fellow cadets had promised him subscriptions for the book. On February 21, Poe wrote to John Allan again. Poe was in New York, very ill with a cold, headache, and ear infection. He was pleading for money, because he was sick, alone, and broke. He accused Allan of letting him get to this point and appealed to his sense of justice, not his affection. Even though he never heard from Allan again, Poe wrote whenever he was at his wit's end, begging for help.

This lithograph paints a pleasant picture of a New York winter on Wall Street. Poe's experience there in February of 1832 was less than pleasurable.

Edgar Allan Poe was considered an elegant, if melancholy, young man.

THE VALLEY OF UNREST

In about April 1831, Poe's third book, *Poems by Edgar A. Poe, Second Edition,* was published in New York. He wrote an introduction about what he believed poetry to be. Poe spent years working on his definition of poetry, but this was his start. He thought that to criticize poetry, you first had to have a yardstick by which to measure it.

Poe's definition was: "A poem, in my opinion, is opposed to a work of science by having, for its *immediate* object, pleasure, not truth. . . ." He lifted this definition from Samuel Taylor Coleridge, a great poet. He wrote in his Biographia Literaria:

[poetry] is opposed to works of science, by proposing for its *immediate* object pleasure, not truth.

There are other examples of Poe lifting others' work. Another poem in his 1831 book was called "A Paean." It later was revised into his famous poem, "Lenore." In "A Paean" Poe wrote:

> How shall the burial rite be read?
> > The solemn song be sung?
> The requiem for the loveliest dead,
> > That ever died so young?

George Darley published a poem called "The Wedding Wake" a few years earlier that includes the very similar lines:

> Be this the funeral song:
> Farewell, the loveliest and the best
> > That ever died so young!

STOLEN WORDS

Poe attacked writers who stole, or plagiarized, other writers' words, but he himself plagiarized many times. Plagiarism often occurs without the writer meaning to steal. He or she remembers something that has been read and uses the words, idea, or meter in his or her own work. Sometimes writers do it on purpose. Poe lifted whole sections of prose and poetry without giving credit to the original authors. In his later work as a critic, he was scathing about writers who didn't use "original" ideas.

Poe's 124-page book included revised versions of "Al Aaraaf" and "Tamerlane." Three of the new poems, "To Helen," "The Doomed City," and "Israfel" are thought to be among his best. They were rewritten over time, as was most of his work. Although critics now find the book interesting and the poetry worthwhile, at the time it didn't get much notice. Its two or three reviews were lukewarm at best. One reviewer wrote in the *Morning Courier and New-York Enquirer*, "He has a fine genius ... and may be distinguished, if he will not mistake oddity for excellence."

Poe had taken subscriptions for his book from the cadets at West Point. When they got the book, many were disappointed. It was small and badly printed on cheap paper. They were probably hoping for something funny or rude. One cadet wrote, "The book was received with a general expression of disgust." The print run of about one thousand copies did not sell out. It was fourteen years before Poe published another book of poetry.

The historic Tamerlane is considered one of the world's greatest conquerors. At the time of his death in 1405, his empire stretched from India to the Mediterranean Sea.

LITTLE OF ANYTHING

Even though Poe had recovered enough to get his book finished and published, he didn't find work in New York. He thought about going to Paris and joining the Polish army. Instead, he went to Baltimore to live with his family. By the beginning of May, he moved into a small house on a street called Mechanics Row. He looked for work but failed to get a job with a newspaper or as a teacher. He started writing short stories. The Philadelphia Saturday Courier ran a contest offering a prize of "ONE HUNDRED DOLLARS to the writer of the best ORIGINAL TALE," and Poe entered five stories.

While Poe was writing and trying to earn money, Maria Clemm was keeping house. Her mother was still unable to move, her son and daughter were young, and Henry Poe was sick. The family had very little money coming in. One neighbor later said, "Mrs. Clemm could make a little of anything go twice as far as other people could." Their house was neat and clean. Maria was good at begging for food, handouts, and small jobs, such as sewing. She was forty-one, and as one person said, "She had the size and figure of a man."

On August 1, 1831, Henry Poe died at the age of twenty-four, probably of alcoholism. He left a debt of eighty dollars that Edgar seems to have taken on. Poe wrote to John Allan on October 16, saying he felt sad that their relationship had ended. He apologized for being ungrateful and for always asking for money. He said that he was now poor, but not in debt, and not asking for money this time. Only a month later, threatened with prison again because of his debts, Poe wrote to Allan for help.

My dear Pa,

I am in the greatest distress and have no other friend on earth to apply to except yourself if you refuse to help me I know not what I shall do. I was arrested eleven days ago for a debt which I never expected to have to pay. . . .

There is no proof that Poe was actually arrested, and there is no record that he ever went to prison. Allan didn't write back. Maria Clemm and Poe each wrote again, begging for money. Finally, in January 1832, Allan silently sent money through a man he knew.

On December 31, 1831, the *Saturday Courier* announced that Delia S. Bacon won its contest. Although Poe didn't win the prize, the *Courier* did go on to publish his five stories during 1832. Poe was probably not paid for them, nor was he named as their author. They were his first published fiction and showed some of his great talents. The best one, "Metzengerstein," is a gothic horror story that has an absurd plot about a nobleman who gives in to evil and rides off on a horse that leaps out of a tapestry. The tone and feeling of terror build toward the ending. Poe based its tone on popular German gothic horror stories of the day. He took the common theme of a strange aristocrat in spooky surroundings and went further, ending up with a gripping horror story. Poe already knew how to use language and grammar to create suspense.

Up the long avenue of aged oaks which led from the forest to the main entrance of the Chateau Metzengerstein, a steed, bearing an unbonneted and disordered rider, was seen leaping with an impetuosity which outstripped the very Demon of the Tempest, and extorted from every stupefied beholder the ejaculation—"horrible."

The career of the horseman was indisputably, on his own part, uncontrollable. The agony of his countenance, the convulsive struggle of his frame, gave evidence of superhuman exertion: but no sound, save a solitary shriek, escaped from his lacerated lips, which were bitten through and through in the intensity of terror. One instant, and the clattering of hoofs resounded sharply and shrilly above the roaring of the flames and the shrieking of the winds—another, and, clearing at a single plunge the gate-way and the moat, the steed bounded far up the tottering staircases of the palace, and, with its rider, disappeared amid the whirlwind of chaotic fire.

The fury of the tempest immediately died away, and a dead calm sullenly succeeded. A white flame still enveloped the building like a shroud, and, streaming far away into the quiet atmosphere, shot forth a glare of preternatural light; while a cloud of smoke settled heavily over the battlements in the distinct colossal figure of—a horse.

FRIENDS AND FAMILY

No one is sure what Poe did between 1832 and 1834. He was probably working hard on his writing. It is possible he was writing for newspapers to earn money while he kept trying to perfect his fiction. He visited friends and most likely had some romances with young women. He didn't have the money to join in Baltimore society, but he did his best to look fashionable. He always displayed good manners and was quite confident. Poe made friends with his cousin Elizabeth Herring. He was also friends with Lambert Wilmer, who wrote for the *Baltimore Saturday Visiter.* In the spring of 1833, Poe's household moved to Amity Street in Baltimore.

At some point during this time, Poe possibly had a romance with a woman named Mary Starr or Mary Deveraux. She described him:

> Mr. Poe was about five feet eight inches tall, and had dark, almost black hair. . . . His eyes were large and full, gray and piercing. . . . He had a sad, melancholy look. He was very slender . . . but had a fine

Poe's house on 203 Amity Street is now a tourist site and museum.

figure, an erect, military carriage, and a quick step. But it was his manner that most charmed. It was elegant. When he looked at you it seemed as if he could read your very thoughts. His voice was pleasant and musical, but not deep.

She claimed he was a jealous man and reported that they argued one night after he had been drinking. She ran into her house, and her mother sent her upstairs and forbade Poe from seeing her again. This seems unlikely, but it may have happened. This same Mary may have seen him years later in New Jersey and at his home in New York, but no one can prove this.

By 1832, John Allan was ill. Poe may have tried to see him in June 1832, but no one is sure. He may have tried again in February 1834. One early biographer said he did see Allan who, "raised his cane" and

In this illustration, the narrator of "MS. Found in a Bottle" is trapped below deck on a harrowing sea journey.

threatened to hit him. On March 27, 1834, Allan died. He left three sons, several illegitimate children, and his second wife. Poe may have tried that May to see Allan's widow, who didn't like him. Allan left Poe nothing in his will, and Poe no longer had any hope of being bailed out when he got into trouble. Although we know him as Edgar Allan Poe, when he was alive he almost always signed his name and his work "Edgar A. Poe."

Poe kept trying to get his work published to earn money. In June 1833, the *Baltimore Saturday Visiter* announced a contest with a prize of "50 dollars for the best Tale and 25 dollars for the best Poem." Poe entered a poem and six stories. His tense horror story "MS. Found in a Bottle" won the prize. Finally, he had a success. His poem "The Coliseum" was also published in the *Visiter.* One of the judges, John Pendleton Kennedy, became Poe's friend. He gave him clothes, invited him for dinner, and let him ride his horses. Kennedy also tried to help him get more work published. In 1835, he helped Poe place work in the *Southern Literary Messenger,* published by Thomas Willis White.

Poe wrote different kinds of stories. Some were satires of things that were important at the time. Some were exaggerated comedies that used silly names and complicated grammar and punctuation to seem funny. The

John Pendleton Kennedy was able to help Edgar Allan Poe climb out of poverty—but not for long. Poe suffered money troubles for much of his remaining life.

This illustration by the famous Arthur Rackham shows the Baron of "Metzengerstein" on his horse.

best were his horror stories. Poe wrote about things that frightened people—about death and fear, family ties, illness, storms, and accidents. Even though most of his stories are too exaggerated or supernatural to be true, they have a ring of truth that makes them believable. His stories started getting noticed and received better reviews.

At the time, people were very interested in death. Many were questioning the Christian belief in an afterlife, and many more were insisting upon it. Poems about meeting dead children, spouses, and parents in heaven were common in newspapers and magazines. People kept hair, shoes, and clothes from loved ones who had died. Poe's writings followed the interest in death, but his works were different. The deaths in his stories and poems weren't clear-cut. Many of his characters were not quite dead or came back to life. The life after death he wrote about was gruesome, not heavenly. In his poem "Visit of the Dead," he wrote:

The spirits of the dead, who stood
In life before thee, are again
In death around thee, and their will
Shall then o'ershadow thee . . .

By the middle of 1835, Poe was offering White advice on the kind of writing he should be publishing. Poe claimed that though people said they wanted simple stories, "take my word for it no one cares any thing about simplicity in their hearts. . . . To be appreciated you must be *read*." He said White should publish stories like his horror tales. Poe went on to say, "I propose to furnish you every month with a Tale of [this] nature." He said more copies of the magazine would sell to prove him right. In the summer of 1835, Poe went to Richmond to work for White on the *Messenger*.

Thomas Willis White entered the printing business at the tender age of eleven. He started the *Southern Literary Messenger* in 1834.

This portrait is supposedly of Virginia Clemm as a young girl.

Moving Around

Edgar Allan Poe got off to a hard start in Richmond in August 1835. His grandmother had died just before he left Baltimore, so Maria Clemm and Virginia had hardly any money coming in. Their main income had been the pension that died with Mrs. Poe. Edgar was worried about how Maria and Virginia would survive. When his cousin Nielson offered to take Virginia in, Poe was horrified. He wrote to Maria on August 29:

> I am blinded with tears while writing this letter . . . I love, you know I love Virginia passionately devotedly. I cannot express in words the fervent devotion I feel towards my dear little cousin—my own darling. . . . It is useless to disguise the truth that when Virginia goes

with N. P. [Nielson Poe] that I shall never behold her again—that is absolutely sure. . . . Can I, in honour & truth say—Virginia! Do not go!—do not go where you can be comfortable & perhaps happy— and on the other hand can I calmly resign my—life itself. . . . What have I *to live for?* Among strangers with *not one soul to love me.* . . . I *cannot advise you.* Ask Virginia. Leave it to her. . . . Kiss her for me— a million times

At the end he added:

For Virginia,
My love, my own sweetest Sissy, my darling little wifey, think well before you break the heart of your own cousin Eddy.

Poe seems to have fallen in love with Virginia some time before. Poe was twenty-six. Virginia had just turned thirteen. She called him Eddie. He called her Sis or Sissy. They both called Maria Muddy. Although they were first cousins, marrying one's cousin was common at the time. Some members of their family had already done so. Girls often married young by today's standards, but thirteen was young even for Poe's time. Poe feared that his family didn't want him to marry Virginia, perhaps because she was his first cousin, perhaps because she was so young.

Poe was lonely and not sure what the future held for him. His position with Thomas White was not very clear. White didn't want to name Poe as editor of the *Southern Literary Messenger,* but Poe was doing the editor's job. He was earning regular, good money. He offered to support Maria and Virginia if they came to live with him in Richmond.

Poe stayed in Richmond until the middle of September but was very upset. He wrote to John Kennedy, "I am suffering under a depression of spirits such as I have never felt before." His writing was getting good reviews, but he was drinking again. By September 22, he was back in Baltimore and got a license to marry Virginia. They probably didn't marry then, but he did convince Maria and Virginia to come to Richmond with him.

BACK IN RICHMOND

White had written to Poe while he was in Baltimore. He said that Poe couldn't work for the *Messenger* if he was going to drink again. White believed that no one should drink alcohol. He said, "No man is safe who drinks before breakfast!" Poe must have convinced him that he wouldn't drink again. By October, Poe, Maria, and Virginia were in Richmond. Poe was working on the *Messenger* again. White later named him as editor.

Living in a boardinghouse and working hard, Poe found his life improving. He wrote to Kennedy on January 22, 1836, "My health is better than for years past, my mind is fully occupied, my pecuniary difficulties [money problems] have vanished, I have a fair prospect of future success—in a word all is right."

Poe published poems and stories. They were mostly reworkings of things he had already written. He was trying unsuccessfully to get his stories published as a book. He started to write reviews. They were often kind, but he became famous for his harsh reviews. He could pull to pieces the grammar, style, and content of someone's work and be merciless with his scorn.

About May 1836, the family moved into a house. On May 16 of that year, Virginia and Edgar were married in Richmond. On the marriage bond it was sworn that Virginia was twenty-one, but she was still thirteen. Poe's friend Lambert Wilmer later described what Poe and Virginia were like with each other: "I never knew him to give her an unkind word, and doubt if they ever had any disagreement. That Virginia loved him, I am quite certain." Poe tutored Virginia to help her learn more about subjects such as math and French. He also bought her a piano when he could afford it and encouraged her to play it and sing.

Even though things were going well, Poe and White were not happy. By the end of 1836, both had been sick. While Poe was editor, the *Messenger* went from selling about 500 copies each month to selling about 3,500. Despite this, White was not happy giving all of the editorial

The marriage certificate of Virginia Clemm and Edgar Allan Poe shows that a witness, Thomas W. Cleland, certified Virginia was twenty-one.

Literary Criticism

A book review usually tells what happens in a story, what kind of tone the author uses, and whether or not the reader liked it. Literary criticism tries to take this one step further. By using standards of what makes a good poem, for example, and knowing about other poetry, a critic should be able to paint a balanced picture of how well the author has written. Looking at the way language and grammar are used is part of literary criticism.

control and decision-making to Poe. By the end of January 1837, Poe was no longer the editor.

DIFFICULT TIMES

In February, the family went to New York and settled in Greenwich Village. Poe had published the beginning of *The Narrative of Arthur Gordon Pym* in the *Messenger* before he left Richmond. He sold the whole story to Harper & Brothers publishers. Before they could introduce it to the public, however, the Panic of 1837 hit. Many people and businesses lost a lot of money. This was the beginning of a long economic depression.

Harpers finally published *Pym* in July 1838. Poe's longest work, it was more than two hundred pages. The book wasn't a success in the United States, although it sold well in England. Because copyright laws were not in place, Poe earned nothing from those sales. The book was fairly well reviewed, but many people weren't sure who had written it. It is presented as a true story, with Poe's name only mentioned casually.

Many readers believed it was true. It is about a man who has a horrible list of adventures and disasters at sea. Poe used a great deal of scientific and descriptive detail. The story runs from terrifying suspense to disgusting descriptions of cannibalism and plague.

> [after doing his best in a storm at sea, with a friend who had passed out in the bottom of the boat, Pym puts his trust in God] Hardly had I come to this resolution when, suddenly, a loud and long scream or yell, as if from the throats of a thousand demons, seemed to pervade the whole atmosphere around and above the boat. Never while I live shall I forget the intense agony of terror I experienced at that moment. My hair stood erect on my head—I felt the blood congealing in my veins—my heart ceased utterly to beat, and without having once raised my eyes to learn the source of the alarm, I tumbled head-long and insensible upon the body of my fallen companion.

We don't know much about this time in Poe's life. There aren't many letters or records about him. We know he probably didn't find much work. It appears that he only published two of his old stories and a long review. The days of having enough money and regular work with the *Messenger* were over. He may have been drinking again. Poe never earned enough to support him for long. They often faced hunger, cold, and desperate poverty. His average earnings translated into today's money would put him below the poverty line.

By the summer of 1838, the family moved to Philadelphia. Despite being smaller than New York, Philadelphia had a strong publishing industry. Poe still found it difficult to find a job. He even tried to get different work, possibly as a clerk or printer. One friend wrote that the family was living "on bread and molasses for weeks together." Many critics have commented on how frequently food is written about in *Pym*. *Pym* is often starving or about to eat odd meals, perhaps because Poe was starving as well.

Poe published a story called "Ligeia" in a Baltimore magazine called the *American Museum* in September 1838. Many think it is one of his best. It is about a man's first wife, named Ligeia, who dies. She then takes over the soul of his second wife, Rowena. When Rowena is about to die, her body turns into Ligeia's as well. It is written with realistic detail, which makes the supernatural subject seem believable.

Poe also published other stories and a poem called "The Haunted Palace." He wrote a textbook on shells. A professor who needed the book written probably hired Poe. Later, he was accused of plagiarizing most of the book.

PHILADELPHIA IN THE EARLY 1800S

In 1840, Philadelphia had a population of 220,000. The city was neatly laid out in a grid. Trees lined the streets. People kept their red brick houses clean and their front steps washed down. There were big city buildings, such as the Navy Yard, Bank of the United States, State House, and Moyamensing Prison. Two colleges and four theaters added spice. Gas lighting and buses made the city feel very modern. There were nine daily newspapers to keep people informed. Although people disagreed over the issue of slavery, Philadelphia was known for its peace and sense of calm.

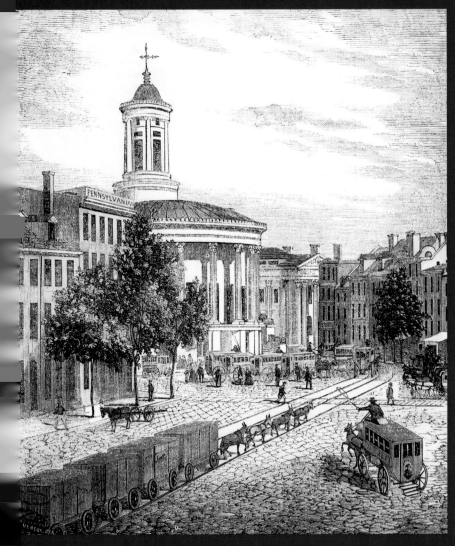

Though Poe found success in Philadelphia, he was not satisfied. The Poe household remained in Philadelphia for little more than five years.

SUCCESS IN PHILADELPHIA

In May 1839, Edgar Allan Poe found a job. William E. Burton, an English actor, had started *Burton's Gentleman's Magazine.* Two years later, Burton needed editorial help. Poe started working as his assistant. He and Burton were listed as editors in the July 1839 issue. Poe was only supposed to work two hours a day but usually worked many more. He was paid enough to feed his family, but they were still poor. Poe wrote many reviews and published his own stories and poems. Many were old ones, but some new work appeared as well. His story "William Wilson" was reprinted in the October 1839 issue after appearing in the anthology *The Gift* a month earlier. It was well reviewed. He wrote puzzles and articles on a range of topics, from gymnastics to Stonehenge. Poe also sold work to other magazines and collections.

Poe's reviews got more critical. Burton asked him to be kinder, but Poe was often very harsh. He later started a long-running battle with Henry Wadsworth Longfellow by accusing him of plagiarizing others' poetry.

One of Poe's most famous stories, "The Fall of the House of Usher," came out in the September 1839 *Burton's Gentleman's Magazine.* The reviewers liked it. One critic, John Frost, said it was "a noble and imposing picture, such as can be drawn only by a master hand." It is an imaginative horror story about a brother and sister who live in a crumbling house. The sister falls into a trance and is sealed into a coffin in a vault. One stormy night the narrator and the brother hear loud thumps. The brother starts raving:

Roderick Usher raves to his friend, the story's narrator, that his sister has risen from her grave.

"Not hear it?—yes, I hear it, and have heard it. Long—long—long—many minutes, many hours, many days, have I heard it—yet I dared not—oh, pity me, miserable wretch that I am!—I dared not—I dared not speak! We have put her living in the tomb! Said I not that my senses were acute? I now tell you that I heard her first feeble movements in the hollow coffin. I heard them—many, many days ago—yet I dared not—I dared not speak! And now—to-night—Ethelred—ha! ha!—the breaking of the hermit's door, and the death-cry of the dragon, and the clangour of the shield!—say, rather, the rending of her coffin, and the grating of the iron hinges of her prison, and her struggles within the coppered archway of the vault! Oh whither shall I fly? Will she not be here anon? Is she not hurrying to upbraid me for my haste? Have I not heard her footsteps on the stair? Do I not distinguish that heavy and horrible beating of her heart? Madman!" here he sprang furiously to his feet, and shrieked out his syllables, as if in the effort he were giving up his soul—"Madman! I tell you that she now stands without the door!"

As if in the superhuman energy of his utterance there had been found the potency of a spell—the huge antique panels to which the speaker pointed, threw slowly back, upon the instant, their ponderous and ebony jaws. It was the work of the rushing gust—but then without those doors there DID stand the lofty and enshrouded figure of the lady Madeline of Usher. There was blood upon her white robes, and the evidence of some bitter struggle upon every portion of her emaciated frame. For a moment she remained trembling and reeling to and fro upon the threshold,—then, with a low moaning cry, fell heavily inward upon the person

Today, Edgar Allan Poe is considered one of the first masters of the short story.

of her brother, and in her violent and now final death-agonies, bore him to the floor a corpse, and a victim to the terrors he had anticipated.

Then the whole house crumbles into ruin. Poe used his poem "The Haunted Palace" in the story. He had written about uncertain death, people rising from graves, madness, and crumbling old mansions before, but this is probably his most accomplished story of that kind. His care with language, realistic detail, and ability to build suspense are masterful.

In December 1839, a collection of twenty-five of Poe's stories was published under the title *Tales of the Grotesque and Arabesque.* The publishers, Lea & Blanchard, only printed 750 copies and didn't think they would make any money on it. Neither did Poe. The two-volume book was mostly well reviewed. It took three years to sell the 750 copies.

A poet who knew Poe described him after he started working for Burton in 1839: "He was clad in a plain and rather worn suit of black which was carefully brushed, and his linen was especially notable for its cleanliness. His eyes at the time were large, bright and piercing, his manner easy and refined, his tone and conversation winning. . . . Mrs. Poe was a delicate gentlewoman, with an air of refinement and good breeding, and Mrs. Clemm had more of the mother than the mother-in-law about her." He went on to say he once found Poe drunk in a gutter and helped him home. He knew of other times when Poe was found drunk in the city. He said this didn't happen often. Poe himself said he hadn't had alcohol for years, except for one time when he was upset.

The family moved many times in Philadelphia but never had enough money to be comfortable. By the end of May 1840, Poe was planning to launch his own magazine. It was to be more expensive and more highbrow than Burton's. Poe planned to call it the *Penn*. He hoped to make a strong literary magazine and also earn more money. Poe and Burton had a big argument, perhaps over money, perhaps over Poe's plans for the *Penn,* perhaps because Burton put his magazine up for sale without telling Poe. Poe no longer worked for Burton after the beginning of June.

Poe printed up selling sheets to try and get subscribers for the *Penn*. He had to have enough people paying five dollars a year to cover his costs before he could publish the first issue. After advertising, mailing his sheets, asking friends and family for help, and getting notice from newspapers and magazines, Poe thought he was ready to bring it out. He promised it in January 1841, but got sick in December and put it off until March. On February 4, 1841, there was another panic in the economy. Poe said he never published the first issue of the *Penn* because of this bank panic.

GRAHAM'S MAGAZINE

On October 20, 1840, Burton sold his magazine to George R. Graham. Graham published a magazine called the *Casket.* He bought Burton's list of 3,500 subscribers. Adding it to his list, Graham now had a total of about 5,000 subscribers. Because each subscriber paid a few dollars for his or her year's subscription, the list of names was very valuable. Graham merged the two magazines into one. He called it *Graham's Lady's and Gentleman's Magazine (The Casket and Gentleman's United).* The first issue came out in November. Poe had a story in that issue. By April 1841, Poe was working on the magazine. He was paid $800 a year. Burton had paid him about $520 a year.

    Graham's Magazine was a huge success. It gave readers a mix of literary stories, horror stories, poetry about happy children, reviews of popular music, illustrations drawn specially for each issue, and pictures of fashions. Graham paid writers and illustrators more than anyone else did.

The publishing venture of George R. Graham became a huge success. Besides Poe's writings, *Graham's Magazine* published works by William C. Bryant, James Fenimore Cooper, and Henry Wadsworth Longfellow.

Magazines in the 1800s

In the early 1800s, more and more Americans learned to read. More could see, too, because eyeglasses got better. Trains could deliver mail, books, and magazines over great distances quickly and reliably. It was a "golden age" for magazines. Between 1825 and 1850, up to five thousand new magazines started. Many failed. By 1840, there were four hundred U.S. magazines. *Godey's Lady's Book* was the first American women's magazine to be a lasting success. It began in 1830 and was published for almost seventy years.

He also only wanted work that hadn't been published anywhere else. By the end of its first year, *Graham's Magazine* had 25,000 subscribers.

Poe didn't choose what went into *Graham's Magazine* as he had with the *Messenger* and *Burton's Gentleman's Magazine*. He wrote reviews, composed puzzles, and checked the proofs before the magazine was printed. He also wrote stories. He was paid extra for his stories. The month he started, he published "The Murders in the Rue Morgue."

People call this the first real detective story. The detective, C. Auguste Dupin, is a withdrawn man living in a mansion in Paris with a friend. He has great analytic powers. His friend tells the story of how Dupin solves a murder in which one of the victims is found in a locked room. Dupin investigates at the crime scene, then advertises for a sailor with a pet orangutan. He says the orangutan was the murderer. He worked it all out from the clues left in the room and from what people nearby had heard. At the time police forces were new. Solving crimes and catching criminals interested people. Poe wrote more stories about his detective. Later, Sir Arthur Conan Doyle based Sherlock Holmes on Poe's Dupin and his ability to analyze details to solve crimes.

POE'S PLANS

Poe still wanted to publish his own magazine. He hoped Graham would help finance it. Like the *Penn,* it would be more literary than the popular *Graham's Magazine.* It would have fewer subscribers and few illustrations. It would mainly feature writers of the "highest talent." Poe's hope died out when nothing happened.

Poe worked hard on the details in his pieces. He rewrote his work many times, even after a piece had been published. He had strong ideas about what made good writing and tried to apply his ideals to his own work. In 1842, he wrote, ". . . we would define in brief the Poetry of words as the *Rhythmical Creation of Beauty.*" Like most writers, he didn't

In "The Murders in the Rue Morgue," two terrible murders are committed by an orangutan as the animal's owner watches in horror from the window.

find writing very easy. He didn't have long, dry stretches when he wrote nothing at all, but he did have periods when he wrote more than usual. He wrote a letter to a friend in 1841, saying, "To coin one's brain into silver . . . is to my thinking, the hardest task in the world." Poe always wrote with the intention of publishing his work. He wanted to make as much money from it as possible. Writing was the only way he knew how to support his family.

At the end of 1841, Poe published "Eleonora" in the *Gift*. It is about a couple who have lived together since they were children in a secluded valley. "We lived all alone, knowing nothing of the world without the valley,—I, and my cousin, and her mother." The cousins fall in love, and everything is wonderful. Even the plants in the valley change because of the strength of their love. Then Eleonora dies young. She is afraid that her cousin will come to love someone else in time. When he does

Eleonora and her cousin live in a natural paradise called the Valley of the Many-Coloured Grass.

indeed fall in love and marry, Eleonora's voice comes to him to tell him that this is all right. Unlike Poe's other stories about women who die, such as "Ligeia," "Eleonora" has no horrifying or suspenseful tone.

Poe was worried about his own cousin at the time he wrote this. Virginia was sick with tuberculosis. She was singing in January 1842 when she started to bleed from her mouth. Doctors thought she would soon die, but she recovered. For the next five years, she had cycles of terrible illness followed by better health. Poe's moods followed her health. When she was very ill, he listened to her cough with "a shudder, a heart-chill that was visible." Poe wrote about this time later, talking about her relapses and recoveries. "Then again—again—again & even once again at varying intervals. Each time I felt all the agonies of her death—and . . . I loved her more dearly & clung to her life. . . . But I am . . . nervous in a very unusual degree. I became insane, with long intervals of horrible sanity. During these fits of absolute unconsciousness I drank, God only knows how often or how much."

Virginia Poe brought great joy to her husband's life, but her illness caused him tremendous anxiety.

By the end of 1842, *Graham's Magazine* was a huge success, with more than forty thousand subscribers. Poe was not happy. He had tried to get a job in Washington, D.C., working in a well-paid government job. That didn't work out.

In March, Poe met Charles Dickens, who was visiting from London. Dickens was wildly popular in the United States. Poe had reviewed his writing. Dickens was impressed by Poe's work. He agreed to try to find an English publisher for him.

In April 1842, Poe left *Graham's Magazine*. He explained this in a letter: "My reason for resigning was disgust with the namby-pamby character of the *Magazine* . . . the contemptible pictures, fashion-plates, music, and love-tales." Still, he and Graham were friends when he left. Poe planned to sell him work, and Graham thought he was a "polished gentleman."

Unlike Poe, Charles Dickens achieved literary success within his lifetime. His early novels, including *Oliver Twist* and *The Pickwick Papers*, made him a celebrity in Great Britain and the United States.

This engraving of Edgar Allan Poe accompanied an 1845 article
profiling him in *Graham's Magazine.* But Poe thought is was an
inferior likeness and wrote, "It scarcely resembles me at all."

FAME BUT NOT FORTUNE

In 1842, Edgar Allan Poe was so broke that he tried unsuccessfully to file for bankruptcy. He was very upset when Virginia was ill and often got sick himself. Even though he was publishing reviews and new stories regularly, the family had hardly any money to live on. They often had to beg for money. Poe tried again to get a government job. He also kept trying to find new backers or partners with whom to publish his own magazine.

It seemed that the only time Poe brought in enough money to live on was when he was working as an editor. Why did these jobs only last a year or so? Perhaps Poe was not the right kind of person to survive as an editor. He was quiet, polite, and gentlemanly. Editors at the time were usually more hardy, loud, and thick-skinned. Despite his reserve, Poe was often violent with his pen in reviews. Some readers found this exciting, but others found it too nasty. He could also be very snobbish, especially when describing his definition of poetry or good writing. He didn't like sentimental, flowery, or religious writing, which were very popular at the time. Even with all these challenges, when Poe edited a magazine, it got more readers. Perhaps his horror stories or his silly puzzles and satires pulled them in.

At the end of 1842, Poe's "The Pit and the Pendulum" came out in the *Gift*. It tells how a man feels while he is being tortured. Poe probably

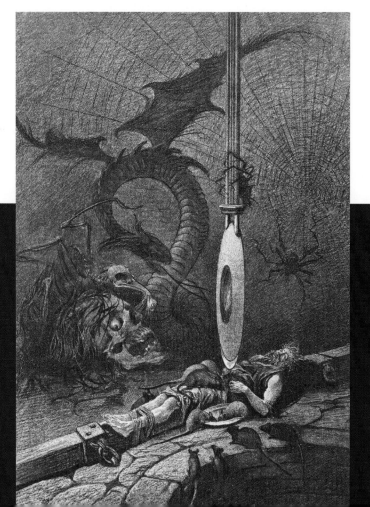

"The Pit and the Pendulum" portrays the psychological horror of torture.

got his ideas for the story from other stories about people who faced terror, darkness, and the Spanish Inquisition. Today, this is probably Poe's most read story. It is chilling in its descriptions of the ordeal and "moral horrors" the prisoner goes through in his cell in the dark. As the sharp pendulum comes down over him, he thinks:

Down—steadily down it crept. I took a frenzied pleasure in contrasting its downward with its lateral velocity. To the right—to the left—far and wide—with the shriek of a damned spirit! to my heart with the stealthy pace of the tiger! I alternately laughed and howled, as the one or the other idea grew predominant.

Down—certainly, relentlessly down! It vibrated within three inches of my bosom! I struggled violently—furiously—to free my left arm. This was free only from the elbow to the hand. I could reach the latter, from the platter beside me to my mouth with great effort, but no farther. Could I have broken the fastenings above the elbow, I would have seized and attempted to arrest the pendulum. I might as well have attempted to arrest an avalanche!

Down—still unceasingly—still inevitably down! I gasped and struggled at each vibration. I shrunk convulsively at its very sweep. My eyes followed its outward or upward whirls with the eagerness of the most unmeaning despair; they closed themselves spasmodically at the descent, although death would have been a relief, O, how unspeakable! Still I quivered in every nerve to think how slight a sinking of the machinery would precipitate that keen glistening axe upon my bosom. It was hope that prompted the nerve to quiver—the frame to shrink. It was HOPE—the hope that triumphs on the rack—that whispers to the death-condemned even in the dungeons of the Inquisition.

Another of Poe's famous stories came out soon after. In January 1843, *Boston Pioneer* magazine published "The Tell-Tale Heart." It tells the story of a murderer who confesses. He is convinced everyone can hear the heartbeat of his victim from where he hid the body, below the floorboards. The murderer thinks in short, sharp sentences, trying to prove he isn't mad but sounding like he is. After the police come, he thinks:

No doubt I now grew VERY pale; but I talked more fluently, and with a heightened voice. Yet the sound increased—and what could I do? It was A LOW, DULL, QUICK SOUND—MUCH SUCH A SOUND AS A WATCH MAKES WHEN ENVELOPED IN COTTON. I gasped for breath, and yet the officers heard it not. I talked more quickly, more vehemently but the noise steadily increased. I arose and argued about trifles, in a high key and with violent gesticulations; but the noise steadily increased. Why WOULD they not be gone? I paced the floor to and fro with heavy strides, as if excited to fury by the observations of the men, but the noise steadily increased. O God! what COULD I do? I foamed—I raved—I swore! I swung the chair upon which I had been sitting, and grated it upon the boards, but the noise arose over all and con-tinually increased. It grew louder—louder—louder! And still the men chatted pleasantly, and smiled. Was it possible they heard not? Almighty God!—no, no? They heard!—they suspected!—they

KNEW!—they were making a mockery of my horror!—this I thought, and this I think. But anything was better than this agony! Anything was more tolerable than this derision! I could bear those hypocritical smiles no longer! I felt that I must scream or die!—and now—again—hark! louder! louder! louder! LOUDER!—

"Villains!" I shrieked, "dissemble no more! I admit the deed!—tear up the planks!—here, here!—it is the beating of his hideous heart!"

Both stories are about horrifying events, but Poe builds that tension even more through the words he uses and the way he constructs sentences.

The illustrations accompanying many of Poe's stories, such as this one for "The Masque of the Red Death," depict gruesome events in a suspenseful and gripping manner.

THE STYLUS

In 1843, Thomas C. Clarke agreed to help Poe finance his magazine. Clarke published the *Saturday Museum,* a popular magazine in Philadelphia. He would put money in but let Poe have editorial control. It would be called *The Stylus,* but otherwise was much the same as the *Penn.*

There are many stories about Poe's life that are inaccurate and many details over which experts argue. After his death, some biographers made up nasty stories about Poe to try and make him sound scandalous and unreliable. Poe started the misinformation in February 1843. His biography and some of his poems were published in the *Saturday Museum.* The article took up the whole front page, in small type. Poe co-wrote the biography and gave details about his life that were incorrect. He said he was two years younger than he really was, came from an aristocratic family, spent more time at school than he did, won prizes he didn't win, wrote works he probably didn't write, went to Russia, and had more literary success than he really did. The details may have been overblown, but the story was hugely popular. It was reprinted on the front page of a later issue.

Poe went to Washington, D.C., to sign up subscribers for *The Stylus* in March 1843. He also wanted to appeal personally to President John Tyler and his son Robert about getting a government job. Poe's trip to Washington was a disaster. He was out of control. He got terribly drunk, became sick, got into a mess, and insulted friends. He wrecked his chances of getting a job in the government, which had been slim anyway because of political wrangling. In May, Clarke pulled out of their project.

At the beginning of 1843, Poe entered a new story in a contest. He won the first prize of one hundred dollars for "The Gold-Bug." It came out in the *Dollar Newspaper* starting on June 21, 1843, and appeared just three days later in the *Saturday Courier.* It is an adventure story about a hunt for treasure following the discovery of a written puzzle. It is set on Sullivan's Island, where Poe was posted in the army. Like he did in his detective stories, Poe makes the way the clues are solved by analysis an exciting part of the story. It was very popular. It was even made into a play a month after it came out. Today, it is considered one of the most popular stories ever published.

The publisher William H. Graham issued *The Prose Romances of Edgar A. Poe* in 1843. It was meant to be Issue One of a long series designed to republish Poe's stories. But it was not a success, and no more issues followed.

During the winter of 1843–1844, Poe lectured on "The Poetry of America." At the time, going to lectures was a popular form of entertainment, like going to the movies is

In "The Gold Bug," an encoded message on a mysterious parchment leads three men to search for pirate treasure.

today. Poe booked six or seven dates in halls in and around Philadelphia. He usually talked for about two hours on poetry and criticism. People were impressed by these lectures and lined up to get in.

BACK TO NEW YORK

In April 1844, Edgar Allan and Virginia Poe decided to move to New York. There doesn't seem to be a good reason for the move. Perhaps Poe

New York in the mid-1800s looked more like a country town than the city it is today. Poe thought the coastline was beautiful.

thought he could make more money and a greater name for himself in a bigger city. They traveled by train and steamboat and arrived in good spirits. Poe found them a boardinghouse and wrote Maria a long, chatty letter. Virginia's health was good, and he was feeling confident.

A few days after arriving, Poe sold a story later called the "Balloon-Hoax" to the *New York Sun*. It is a tale about crossing the Atlantic Ocean in three days by hot-air balloon. People were so excited by the story that they mobbed the newspaper's offices to get copies. They thought it was a real story and wanted to read all the details.

In May, Maria joined the Poes in New York. They moved out of Greenwich Village to board with a farming family on the northern tip of Manhattan. Poe wanted the peace of the country and probably wanted

NEW YORK THROUGH POE'S EYES

When he got to New York, Poe wrote a series of articles about the city for readers in Columbia, Pennsylvania. This is what he saw from his boat as he rowed himself around Manhattan:

> The chief interest of the adventure lay in the scenery of the Manhattan shore, which is here particularly picturesque. . . . I could not look on the magnificent cliffs, and stately trees, which at every moment met my view, without a sigh for their inevitable doom—inevitable and swift. In twenty years, or thirty at farthest, we shall see here nothing more romantic than shipping, ware-houses, and wharves.

Poe's infamous attacks on Henry Wadsworth Longfellow (above) nearly ruined his own reputation.

to save money as well. He was selling stories, but once again was not earning much. He published only one poem in 1844, "Dreamland."

Sometime by the end of 1844, Poe started working for the *New York Evening Mirror* and the *New York Weekly Mirror.* These newspapers were edited by Nathaniel Parker Willis and George Pope Morris. Poe wrote mostly small bits of filler copy. He earned regular money but wrote little that he considered worthwhile. He did write a review of a book edited by Henry Wadsworth Longfellow that began a long conflict between the two writers. People who knew Poe said he seemed depressed and had little hope for the future.

During this time, Poe wrote his most famous poem, "The Raven." It is about a man grieving for a woman he loves who has died. The raven, an omen of death, arrives at his door. It only says, "Nevermore," and will not go away. Poe's lyrical rhythm and carefully chosen words make this a powerful poem. When it was published in the *New York Evening Mirror* on January 29, 1845, "The Raven" was an immediate success. *The New World* said, "Everyone reads the Poem and praises it." The *American Review* published it in February. At the end of February, Poe lectured again, and about three hundred people came to listen. People wrote parodies of his poem, and everyone seemed to know it. Poe was finally famous. He had been well known among publishers, editors, authors, and literary types, but not by the general public. He now had followers and supporters from that group, as well.

While he was popular, Poe got a better job. He became coeditor of the *Broadway Journal,* a new magazine he had written for. The other editors were John Bisco, Charles F. Briggs, and musical editor Henry C. Watson. Starting in February, Poe was given one-third of the profits and had to write at least one page a week. One of Poe's fellow workers on the *Journal* wrote this about him: "Poe was a quiet man about the office, but was uniformly kind and courteous to everyone, and . . . would grow cheerful and even playful." Poe republished many of his old stories and poems and wrote new material as well. He also wrote reviews of books and plays.

Poe started in on Longfellow again with a badly written series of articles. Longfellow never wrote back to defend himself. Poe lost some friends because of how savagely he attacked Longfellow. Most of his accusations were plainly untrue. People thought Poe had become obsessed with the topic of plagiarism.

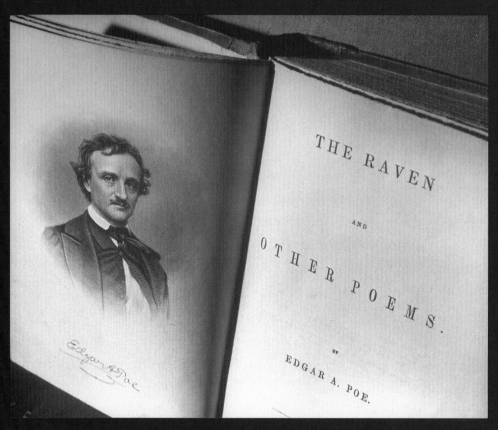

Though Poe's poem "The Raven" was a huge smash, it did not help the sales of his 1845 publication *The Raven and Other Poems*. Poe's writing, even when well received, was never lucrative.

NINE

Many Irons in the Fire

Edgar Allan Poe had been making a 10-mile (16-km) round trip commute to work each day. He probably walked because he couldn't afford any other form of transportation. The family moved in the spring of 1845 to East Broadway so he could be closer to work. Virginia's health went up and down, and Poe was drinking off and on.

In March 1845, Poe met Frances Sargent Osgood, a poet he had published at *Graham's Magazine*. Osgood was married to a painter. She described meeting Poe: "With his proud and beautiful head erect, his dark eyes flashing with the electric light of feeling and of thought, a peculiar, an inimitable blending of sweetness and hauteur in his expression and manner, he greeted me." They became good friends. They wrote poems to each other with a kind of romantic yearning. Although people gossiped about their relationship, Virginia knew about and approved of their friendship. She thought Osgood stopped Poe from drinking.

It was a busy year. In May, Poe wrote to his friend Frederick Thomas:

> The fact is, that being seized, of late, with a fit of industry, I put so many irons in the fire all at once, that I have been quite unable to get them out. For the last three or four months I have been working 14 or 15 hours a day—hard at it all the time . . . And yet, Thomas, I have made no money. I am as poor now as ever I was in my life—except in hope . . .

In July, Briggs left the *Journal*. Poe became its sole editor. Bisco became responsible for its finances. They shared the profits equally. Poe kept publishing in other places as well. That same month, *Graham's Magazine* published "The Imp of the Perverse." It tells how a person will do the one thing that they most wish not to do out of a spirit of perversity. Many people think this story explains Poe's own actions.

Poe also wrote about mesmerism, a kind of hypnotism. It was a mix of science and spiritualism. People thought it could stop death the moment death is about to take hold. Poe's made-up stories about mesmerized people were believed by some to be scientific reports.

In June 1845, Wiley and Putnam of New York published Poe's next book. It was called *Tales*. Poe didn't pick the twelve stories that went into it, and he complained that they were not well chosen. The book was well reviewed in the United States and England. Poe said about 1,500 copies were sold that year. He got eight cents for each copy, which sold for fifty cents. Because the book did well, Wiley and Putnam decided to publish a collection of Poe's poems. *The Raven and Other Poems* came out in November 1845. There were thirty poems, all chosen by Poe. He wrote a preface that said, "With me poetry has been not a purpose, but a passion." It was not as well received and sold few copies.

About September, the family moved to Amity Street near Washington Square Park. Poe started meeting members of literary society around this time. Writers, publishers, and admirers gathered in different people's homes. One lady explained why Poe liked coming to these parties: "He delighted in the society of superior women." Sometimes Virginia came along as well. She was described as "always animated and vivacious." When Poe was asked to recite his work, he usually would. He talked with people and studied them. This is how he got material for a series of sketches he wrote on "The Literati," or literary people. These were published in *Godey's Lady's Book* during 1846. They caused an uproar because they both praised and insulted those people. Godey's had to do reprints to meet the demand for the issue.

Frances Sargent Osgood was one of many "superior women" who attracted the attention of Edgar Allan Poe.

In October, Poe was invited to read a poem in Boston. He couldn't write a new one for the occasion. His turn to speak came after a long lecture. He decided to read "Al Aaraaf." The poem is long and complicated, not catchy like "The Raven." Many in the audience were bored and left. At the end, Poe did read "The Raven." He got drunk afterwards. He wrote a defensive and pompous article about the reading. He tried to make it sound as if he had planned to show the Boston audience to be dull and uneducated. He also put Boston down as a place with bad hotels, bad poetry, and a lot of frogs. He started calling the people who lived in Boston "Frogpondians."

Poe once claimed Boston proudly as his hometown. By the mid-1840s, he fiercely hated the city and the people who lived there.

A MAGAZINE AT LAST

In October 1845, one of Poe's dreams came true. He agreed to buy the *Broadway Journal* from Bisco for fifty dollars. The October 25 issue announced "Edgar A. Poe, Editor and Proprietor." Poe also had to take on its debts. Because he was so poor, it was hard to find enough money to keep it going. He had to keep borrowing fairly large amounts from friends and businesspeople he knew. He wrote to a friend, "I will make a fortune of it." He did a good job getting more advertisers and got the issues published. It was hard work to keep writing, edit it, and manage the financial part of the business as well. He had to bring in a partner, Thomas H. Lane, to help him. Poe got sick, perhaps because the stress was so great. He finally couldn't keep the finances going and had to give up. The January 3, 1846, issue announced that it would be the last. Lane closed down the *Journal* while Poe recovered.

Managing his own publication proved too difficult for the unhealthy Edgar Allan Poe. He kept editorial control for less than three months before the journal shut down.

In 1846, Poe kept writing, mostly articles and reviews. He suffered long periods of illness during which he couldn't write at all. He published few stories, and the family had very little money coming in. One of his most famous stories, "The Cask of Amontillado," came out in *Godey's* in November. It is about a man who gets revenge by sealing his enemy alive in the wine vaults below his family home. The idea is horrible, and the way the story is told makes it even more chilling. The narrator is very calm and sounds reasonable, even while he is building the brick wall to contain his victim.

During 1846, Virginia's health grew worse. She wrote Poe a Valentine's Day poem, which is probably the only poem she ever wrote. It spells out his name and begins:

> Ever with thee I wish to roam—
> Dearest my life is thine.
> Give me a cottage for my home
> And a rich old cypress vine,
> Removed from the world with its sin and care

The Poes left the city soon after and moved to Turtle Bay. Poe briefly visited Baltimore that spring. In May, the family moved again to a cottage in Fordham, about 13 miles (21 km) north of the city, in the Bronx. Poe was often ill himself that year, and he may have hoped the country air in Fordham would help them both feel better. One visitor said the cottage was run down but very neat and clean, surrounded by lawns and cherry trees. Maria wrote, "Oh, how supremely happy we were in our dear cottage home! We three lived only for each other."

Poe's sister, Rosalie, visited for about a month but didn't feel very welcomed into the close family.

GOING TO COURT

After writing his "Literati" pieces, Poe was featured in a satire in the same style he had used. The *Mirror* published the satire and later an article criticizing Poe. In July 1846, Poe decided to sue the *Mirror* for libel, or publishing a statement that attacked him. It took until February 1847 for Poe to win the suit. He was awarded $225. During the trial, his reputation was harmed. Many people attacked him for being insane, drunk, or just unable to take the kind of attacks he himself made. All the attention made him famous in France, where people praised his stories.

In June 1846, Poe wrote a letter to Virginia, ". . . I should have lost my courage *but for you*—my little darling wife. You are my *greatest*

TUBERCULOSIS

Tuberculosis is a disease caused by bacteria. It is transmitted to other people through the air when a patient coughs, sneezes, or talks. It makes tiny lumps grow in otherwise healthy organs, most often the lungs. Patients can be sick for a long time before dying. As their lungs get worse, they frequently cough up blood and become very weak. In the early 1800s, there were no cures for it, and most sufferers died. In the mid-1800s, sick people started going to special hospitals in the country to rest, eat well, and get fresh air. This cured many. Later, doctors tried to help by operating on the diseased lungs. Tuberculosis is now cured with antibiotics.

and *only* stimulus now, to battle with this . . . unsatisfactory, and ungrateful life." Sadly, Poe was soon going to lose Virginia. Mary Gove visited Fordham and described Virginia. "Her pale face, her brilliant eyes, and her raven hair gave her an unearthly look. One felt that she was almost a disrobed spirit, and when she coughed it was made certain that she was rapidly passing away." She visited again in the autumn and wrote, "The weather was cold. . . . She lay on the straw bed, wrapped in her husband's great-coat, with a large tortoise-shell cat on her bosom. . . . The coat and the cat were the sufferer's only means of warmth, except as her husband held her hands, and her mother her feet."

The Fordham cottage opened as a museum in 1917 and is furnished in the style of the 1840s.

Appalled by the state of poverty the Poes were living in, Gove helped raise money and collect blankets and clothes for them. She got Marie Louise Shew to assist with nursing. Newspapers and magazines began to publish stories about how badly the Poes needed help, and people sent them money. Virginia died from tuberculosis on January 30, 1847. She was twenty-four years old. Shew bought her coffin and gave her linen to be buried in.

After the funeral, Poe rested and worked. Maria had just lost her last child. She said that she "wished to die . . . but *had* to live to take care of . . . poor disconsolate Eddie." Maria and Poe thought of each other as mother and son even more than before. Poe was very upset. He was ill with "brain fever" and an irregular heartbeat. Still, he kept working and published a poem and a story in March. The poem was a thank-you tribute to Shew.

Poe's cottage was remembered fondly by Maria Clemm, though it was also the scene of her daughter's demise.

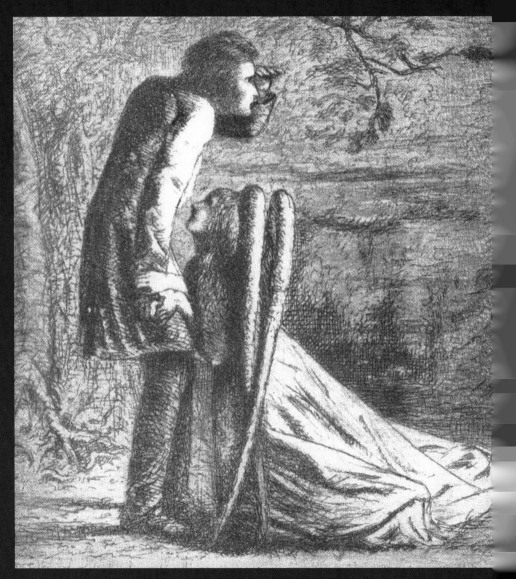

Edgar Allan Poe wrote "Ulalume" while mourning the death of Virginia.

TEN

TRUE AND TENDER

For Edgar Allan Poe, 1847 was a year of recovery. After the stress of Virginia's illness and death, he took some time off to steady himself. There was little money coming in because he did not write or publish much. Many publishers were angry with him because of his libel suit against the *Mirror*. At the beginning of 1847, Poe found out that the *Saturday Evening Post* had accused him of plagiarism. The paper had said that Poe's book about shells was not his own work. Poe decided not to sue.

Poe's poem "Ulalume" came out in the *American Review* in December 1847. Poe thought it was his best, but many others didn't understand it. It is about a man who accidentally visits the grave of his dead love a year after she was buried. There are references to stars and spirits, planets and ghosts. It shows a great deal of sadness and conflict about losing a person so deeply loved.

Poe had been working long and hard on a complicated piece explaining the universe. *Eureka: A Prose Poem* started as a lecture he gave in February 1848. Wiley & Putnam published the book in March. It is a mixture of science, theology, and intuition. Poe puts forward a kind of Big Bang theory that God existed before matter. God created the first atoms. They scattered to create the universe. They are all trying to join back together, but when they do, they will be scattered again. Similarly, people die and are reborn, joining with God. Some people were very upset by his theories, because they were not Christian. Some thought they were brilliant, showing insight and clear thought. Many others were simply confused by them.

At the end of 1848, Poe published the "Rationale of Verse" in the *Southern Literary Messenger*. He explained his theory of poetry, rhythm, and meter. It had been part of an earlier published essay that he revised in 1846 but took a long time to sell. The editor who published it said, "It is altogether too bizarre and too technical for the general reader."

Poe courted Sarah Helen Whitman in the last months of 1848, but the romance ended badly.

In January 1848, Poe wrote to a friend that he wanted to start work on his own magazine, *The Stylus,* again. He said in the same letter, "My health is better—best. I have never been so well." At the end of February, he wrote the same friend, "I rise early, eat moderately, drink nothing but water, and take abundant and regular exercise in the open air. . . . The causes which maddened me to the drinking point are no more, and I am done drinking forever." That spring, however, he got drunk and seemed very ill and distracted. He saw Marie Louise Shew a number of times. She visited him and helped him when he was ill or arrived drunk at her home. She asked doctors for their opinions, and they said his heart was weak. In June, she broke off their friendship. She thought he was too eccentric for them to remain close.

NEW WOMEN

After losing the friendship of Shew, Poe felt very strongly that he needed a wife to help him through life. Maria was looking after him, and he loved her, but he wrote, "Unless some true and tender and pure womanly love saves me, I shall hardly last a year longer, alone!"

Sarah Helen Whitman wrote Poe a poetic valentine in 1848. It was delivered to him by mutual friends. Helen, as she was known, was a well-known poet and critic. She lived in Providence, Rhode Island. Poe and Whitman had admired each other's work for years before she made contact. They wrote back and forth without admitting who they were, though each knew the other's identity.

In July 1848, Poe went to Lowell, Massachusetts, to give a lecture on the poets and poetry of the United States. He had been invited by

Mrs. Jane Locke, a poet he thought to be a widow. They had flirted through letters. She turned out to be married with five children. Locke introduced Poe to her neighbor, Mrs. Nancy Richmond, whom he called Annie. Poe was very attracted to Annie. She said, "He seemed so *unlike* any other person, I had ever known, that I could not think of him in the same way—he was incomparable—not to be measured by any ordinary standard." Annie was also married, with one child.

Later in July, Poe went to Richmond. He was trying to get subscribers for *The Stylus*. He probably saw his sister, Rosalie. He was reported to be drunk at times, trying to explain *Eureka* to people in bars. He may have had a duel with John M. Daniel over an insult in his paper. He met Elmira Royster Shelton, the woman he had first been engaged to in Richmond before he went to the University of Virginia. She was now a widow. They were happy to meet again. Poe thought about asking her to marry him.

In September, Poe decided to go to Whitman's house in Providence. She was a widow who lived with her mother and mentally ill sister. Poe wrote that he fell suddenly in love. "I grew faint with the luxury of your voice and blind with the voluptuous lustre of your eyes." He asked her to marry him. She didn't reply at first. Later she wrote that she was not healthy enough to marry him. He wrote back that he would care for her, comfort and soothe her. She was not convinced. Friends had told her that Poe had "no principle—no moral sense." Poe said he did. Poe had claimed that Whitman was his "first and only" love, which sounds like a lie given how much he loved Virginia. But he wrote, "My soul is incapable of dishonor."

In October, Poe went back to Providence. He again asked Whitman to marry him. She did not answer right away. Then he went to Lowell and had a quarrel with Jane Locke. Poe stayed with the Richmonds. He turned his focus to Annie, holding her hand by the fire. She was married, but he said he loved her like a brother. When Whitman sent Poe a note with no answer in it, Annie told him he should try harder to get Whitman to marry him. Poe set off again for Providence.

On November 4, Poe was in Providence but was very upset. He had a "long, long, hideous night of despair." He didn't go to see Whitman. Instead he bought laudanum, a drug made from opium. He went to Boston, wrote a letter to Annie saying he was miserable, and took half the laudanum. He meant to kill himself but took too much laudanum. His stomach couldn't cope with it, and he vomited it out. He was very ill afterwards. On November 7, he went back to Providence to see Whitman.

Mrs. Nancy Richmond, whom Poe called Annie, encouraged him to pursue other women. They remained close friends until his death.

Poe again asked her to marry him. He pleaded with her to save him. He grew more upset and mentally unbalanced. He went to a friend's house to be nursed back to health for a few days. Finally, Whitman agreed to marry Poe if he gave up drinking forever. Poe went back to New York. Whitman's mother was not happy. She asked Whitman to make sure Poe could not get any of her money or property if they did marry. Poe and Whitman both seemed unsure whether their marriage would go ahead.

THE END OF THE AFFAIR

Poe went to Providence twice in December. The second time, he gave a lecture on poetry. It was very good, and Whitman was flattered by the poems Poe read, which were clearly meant for her. A couple of days later, however, Poe went to her house after having had a bit to drink. Although Whitman was displeased, she forgave him when he returned the next morning. The pair agreed to marry the next week. Then Whitman had a change of heart. She called the wedding off and collapsed into a near-unconscious state. Poe went back to New York. The affair was over after a confusing few months that left both feeling weak.

Poe kept writing Annie letters, declaring his love for her. Her husband was upset, and she wrote to him that she wanted to end their friendship. Poe reported that he was "*deeply* wounded." They kept writing. Most of Annie's family really liked Poe and enjoyed his visits. The Richmonds and Lockes had arguments because of Poe. Poe wanted to move with Maria to a cottage near them, but this never happened.

After Poe had recovered his strength, he started writing again. He wrote to a friend, "Literature is the most noble of professions." In February, he composed one of his most famous poems, "The Bells." Shew said she had helped him start it in 1848. He also wrote the poem "For Annie," which he sent to her before it was published. Another of Poe's best-known poems, "Annabel Lee," and a sentimental sonnet of tribute to Maria Clemm, "To My Mother," were written early in 1849. He wrote a number of stories, such as "Hop-Frog," a story about a jester getting horrible revenge on a mean king. He published some reviews and essays as well. Despite this output, he was as broke as always.

"Annabel Lee" is a fine example of Poe's musical writing. Critics continue to debate whom the poem is about:

> I was a child and she was a child,
> In this kingdom by the sea;
> But we loved with a love that was more than love—
> I and my Annabel Lee—
>
> . . .
>
> The angels, not half so happy in Heaven,
> Went envying her and me—
> Yes! That was the reason (as all me know,
> In this kingdom by the sea)
> That the wind came out of the cloud, chilling
> And killing my Annabel Lee.

Both "Annabel Lee" and "The Bells" were not published until after Poe died.

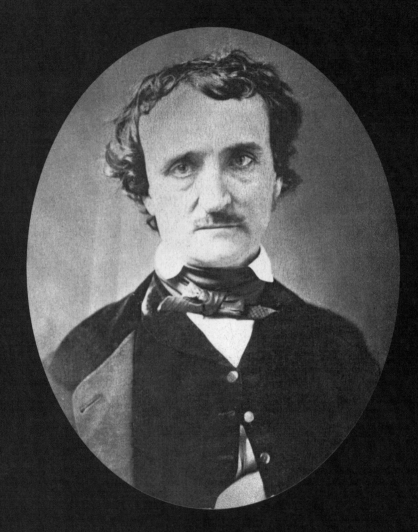

Edgar Allan Poe's last years were difficult and painful. Still, he managed to produce some of his finest poems, including "The Bells" and "Annabel Lee," in his final year of life.

ELEVEN

NEVERMORE

In the spring of 1849, Edgar Allan Poe wrote to Annie Richmond, "Nothing cheers or comforts me. My life seems wasted—the future looks a dreary blank." He was often ill and generally depressed. In April, he got an offer from a young publisher, Edward H. N. Patterson of Oquawka, Illinois. Patterson wanted to help him publish a magazine. They discussed and agreed what it would look like. Poe set off at the end of May on a trip to get subscribers for the new *Stylus*.

After a visit to Lowell and Annie, Poe went back to New York. He needed money from Patterson before he could head for Richmond and then tour the South and West getting subscribers. He finally set off on June 29, 1849. Maria Clemm saw him off on the steamboat to Philadelphia. He said to her, ". . . do not fear for your Eddy[.] See how

DEADLY CHOLERA

Cholera struck quickly. Many of those who got sick with it died, often in just one day. Patients got diarrhea and cramps, and vomited. Passed to people in dirty water, the disease moved quickly through crowded cities. No one knew how to stop it or even control it. Then, in 1849, William Budd and John Snow discovered that cholera was caused by tiny bacteria in water. Cities started building good sewers and supplying clean water. Slowly, epidemics of cholera became less common.

good I will be while I am away from you, and will come back to love and comfort you." When Poe got to Philadelphia, a cholera epidemic had started, and he became ill.

No one knows what really happened in Philadelphia. Poe was sick and mentally disturbed. He may have been drinking or had cholera. He took a medicine made from mercury, which probably made him sicker. He might have gone to Moyamensing Prison and probably saw John Sartain, an editor he knew. Sartain said Poe was having delusions. Sartain was worried that Poe was going to kill himself.

Poe wrote to Maria on July 7, "It is no use to reason with me now; I must die." Maria had been very worried about him, for she had heard nothing since he had left New York. This letter, telling her he had been ill and in prison, couldn't have cheered her up much. His next two letters were also hysterical and depressed in tone. He wanted to see her again but was sure she was dead. On July 19, he wrote to her from

Richmond. It was a much more normal letter. Of his past letters he said, "I was totally deranged." He told her not to lose heart.

In Richmond, Poe tried not to drink but still had a few drunken episodes. He probably suffered from alcohol withdrawal symptoms at least once. In late August, he joined the Sons of Temperance and pledged never to drink again. He saw friends and tried to get his strength back. He lectured on poetry, and met with his sister, Rosalie, and with Elmira Royster Shelton again. He went to Norfolk to lecture as well.

According to Shelton, Poe asked her to marry him. While she didn't say yes absolutely, she said there was a "partial understanding" that they would marry. Poe wrote to Maria on September 18, 1849, about Shelton. "I think she loves me more devotedly than any one I ever knew & I cannot help loving her in return. Nothing is as yet definitely settled—and it will not do to hurry matters. . . . *If possible* I will get married before I start [for New York the following week]." Shelton also wrote to Maria on September 22. She introduced herself and told Maria that Poe was well and that his lectures were very popular. She said Poe spoke "very affectionately" about Virginia. She said nothing about marrying Poe, but she wrote, "I am fully prepared to *love* you."

In 1849, Poe again planned to marry Elmira Royster Shelton, whom he'd been engaged to twenty-three years before!

On September 24, Poe gave his last public lecture on poetry. Two days later, he went to see Shelton the evening before he left for New York. She said he had a fever and felt sick. Other friends who saw him that evening said he seemed "cheerful and sober." He left on the 4 A.M. steamboat for Baltimore on September 27. He may have stopped in Philadelphia, but no one is entirely sure.

THE END

On October 3, there was an election in Baltimore. That day, Poe was found by Joseph Walker, a printer, outside a polling station that was in a bar in Baltimore. Poe was oddly dressed in clothes that were too thin for the weather. He was only semiconscious. Poe told Walker to send for Dr. Joseph E. Snodgrass, a doctor he knew who lived nearby. Snodgrass came to help. Poe's uncle by marriage, Henry Herring, came as well. The two men decided to send Poe to a hospital.

Edgar Allan Poe spent his last days at Washington Medical College in Baltimore.

Poe arrived by carriage at Washington Medical College at 5 P.M. Dr. John J. Moran, who knew and respected Poe's work, took over his care. Poe was unconscious until 3 A.M., when he became delirious and started talking. He was very sad. He talked to "imaginary objects on the walls." Poe's cousin Nielson came to visit but wasn't allowed to see Poe. By Saturday, October 6, 1849, Poe was raving and calling out someone's name. It may have been "Reynolds." Early on Sunday morning, he rested. At about 5 A.M. he said, "Lord help my poor soul" and died. He was forty years old.

No one knows what caused Poe's final illness. It may have been alcohol or exposure to the cold. He was buried the next day, October 8, with little ceremony. Nielson Poe, Henry Herring, Reverend Clemm, Elizabeth Herring and her husband, Dr. Snodgrass, Poe's teacher Joseph Clarke, and Z. Collins Lee, a friend from the University of Virginia, were the only ones there. Colonel J. Alden Weston was walking by and stopped to watch the funeral. He said, "The burial ceremony, which did not occupy more than three minutes, was so cold-blooded and unchristianlike as to provoke on my part a sense of anger difficult to suppress."

Maria Clemm found out about Poe's death through a newspaper report the next day. She wrote to Nielson Poe to confirm the story. She also wrote to Annie to tell her the news. Maria was very upset. She felt very alone, with no one "to cling to and love." Maria moved in with Annie two weeks later. For the rest of her life, she moved around, living with friends. She was often ill and seldom happy. She spent her last years in a nursing home that was housed in the building that had held the Washington Medical College. She died there, in the same building Poe died in, on February 16, 1871, at age eighty-one.

POE'S LEGACY

Poe made little money from his writing during his life. Maria, who inherited his estate, made little after his death. Rosalie briefly hired a lawyer to try and get the rights to inherit Poe's estate but gave up her claim quickly. Rufus W. Griswold, a writer and editor who had replaced Poe on *Graham's Magazine,* was Poe's literary executor. That means he was in charge of sorting out Poe's written work.

Griswold and Poe had met in 1841, when Griswold used three of Poe's poems in a book he was editing, *The Poets and Poetry of America.* In his reviews, Poe had attacked Griswold's writing and editorial choices. Poe and Griswold were not friends. In fact, Griswold may have wanted to get even with him. On October 9, 1849, Griswold published a notice of Poe's death in the *New York Tribune.* He said Poe was a great and skilled author. He also wrote:

> This announcement will startle many, but few will be grieved by it. . . . he had few or no friends . . . He walked the streets, in madness or melancholy, with lips moving in indistinct curses . . . with a face shrouded in gloom, he would brave the wildest storms; and all night, with drenched garments and arms wildly beating the wind and rain, he would speak as if to spirits . . .

Other papers and magazines published more balanced portraits of Poe. That same day, the *New York Journal of Commerce* wrote, "Few men were his equals. He stands in a position among our poets and prose writers which has made him the envy of many and the admiration of all. His life has been an eventful and stormy one . . . " Poe's friends and admirers added their own obituaries. Griswold, however, continued building up an exaggerated picture of this mad, wild man by publishing made-up stories and letters. People believed what Griswold wrote because he was Poe's official biographer. Griswold edited volumes of Poe's stories, poems, and articles. The first one had biographical articles as well. The first two volumes came out in January 1850.

Many of the people who had known Poe wrote about him as well. Often, these stories contradicted each other. Some of them were written many years later, so the writers may have forgotten details. Poe himself told many inaccurate tales about his life. As time went on, the picture of him as a depressed, drunk, mad adventurer grew to be more accepted than his true story. Modern biographers have put a lot of effort

Every year since 1949, a mysterious stranger has left a tribute of cognac and white roses by Poe's gravesite.

into untangling truth from fiction, but many details are still not clear.

Over time, Poe's work grew more famous, not just because of its strengths, but because of what it inspired. Many people think Poe began the genre of science fiction. His detective C. Auguste Dupin inspired Sir Arthur Conan Doyle to create Sherlock Holmes. The Dupin stories began the genre of detective stories. His work stands on its own as well. The atmosphere and tension that Poe's poems and stories evoke are still as fresh today as they were more than 150 years ago. In 1850, George W. Peck perhaps put it best: "Instead of avoiding the shadow, he would boldly walk into it and analyse it."

Edgar Allan Poe explored the dark places of the human heart—pain, melancholy, horror— but never despaired of mankind's ability to love and appreciate what is beautiful.

TIMELINE

EDGAR ALLAN POE 'S LIFE   WORLD EVENTS

1809 Edgar Poe is born on January 19 in Boston.

1811 Elizabeth Poe, Edgar's mother, dies in Richmond, Virginia, on December 8. Sometime, most likely before then, his father, David Poe, dies. Edgar is taken in by his foster parents, John and Frances Allan. His brother, William Henry, and sister, Rosalie, are cared for by different families.

1812 The War of 1812 begins between the United States and Britain.

1814 Edgar starts school.

The War of 1812 ends.

1815 The Allan family moves to London.

1816 Edgar goes to boarding school.

1820 The Allan family moves back to Richmond.

1821 Edgar starts school in Richmond.

1825 John Allan inherits his uncle's fortune and becomes rich.

The Erie Canal, a waterway linking the Hudson River to Lake Erie, is opened.

1826 Edgar gets engaged to Elmira Royster. He goes to the University of Virginia and runs up large debts, particularly because of gambling.

1827 Edgar leaves home and moves to Boston. His first book of poetry, *Tamerlane, and Other Poems,* is published. He joins the army on May 26 under the name Edgar A. Perry. His battery moves to South Carolina.

1828 Poe's battery moves to Virginia.

1829 Poe is promoted to sergeant major. Poe leaves the army on April 15. He applies to the U.S. Military Academy at West Point. Poe settles in Baltimore near his biological relatives. In December, his second book, *Al Aaraaf, Tamerlane, and Minor Poems,* is published.

1830 Poe moves back to Richmond in January. He leaves for West Point in May.

President Andrew Jackson signs the Indian Removal Act, which orders thousands of Native Americans to be forced from their lands.

1831 Poe is dismissed from West Point on February 19 after refusing to go to classes. Poe moves to New York. His third book comes out in April, *Poems by Edgar A. Poe, Second Edition.* Poe moves to Baltimore by May and lives with his family in poverty. On August 1, his brother dies.

1832 Poe's first stories are published in magazines.

1833 In October, Poe wins first prize in a contest run by the *Baltimore Saturday Visiter* with his story "MS. Found in a Bottle."

1834 John Allan dies on March 27.

1835 In August, Poe goes to Richmond to work on the *Southern Literary Messenger.* Poe's aunt Maria Clemm and cousin Virginia Clemm move in with him in Richmond in October.

1836 Poe marries thirteen-year-old Virginia on May 16.

Texas declares its independence from Mexico.

1837 In January, Poe leaves the *Messenger.* The family moves to New York.

1838 The family moves to Philadelphia in the summer. *The Narrative of Arthur Gordon Pym* is published in July. "Ligeia" is published.

1839 Poe writes his book on shells. In May, he starts as an editor for the *Burton's Gentleman's Magazine.* In September, "The Fall of the House of Usher" is published. In December, his book of stories *Tales of the Grotesque and Arabesque* is published.

1840 In the spring, Poe starts planning his own magazine. He leaves the *Burton's Gentleman's Magazine.*

1841 In April, Poe starts working on *Graham's Magazine.* He publishes "The Murders in the Rue Morgue" and "Eleanora."

1842 In April, Poe leaves *Graham's Magazine.* "The Pit and the Pendulum" is published.

1843 "The Tell-Tale Heart" is published. Poe finds a partner to publish his own magazine, now called *The Stylus.* Poe meets Charles Dickens. Poe wins first prize in a contest run by the *Dollar Newspaper* for his story "The Gold-Bug." *The Prose Romances of Edgar A. Poe* is published. Poe starts lecturing on poetry.

1844 The family moves to New York in the spring. Poe published the "Balloon-Hoax" and "Dreamland." He starts working for the *New York Evening Mirror* and *New York Weekly Mirror.* He begins his feud with Henry Wadsworth Longfellow.

1845 "The Raven" is published in January and makes Poe famous. Poe becomes an editor of the Broadway Journal in February. He is the sole editor by July. *Tales* is published. In October, he buys the Broadway Journal. In November, *The Raven and Other Poems* is published.

1846 In January, Poe closes down the Broadway Journal. "The Cask of Amontillado" is published. Poe sues the *Mirror* for libel.

The Mexican War begins.

1847 Poe's wife, Virginia, dies from tuberculosis on January 30. His poem "Ulalume" is published.

1848 Poe lectures on the universe in February. In June, *Eureka: A Prose Poem* is published. Poe starts working on publishing his own magazine again. Poe becomes involved with Sarah Helen Whitman. Whitman agrees to marry him after a short courtship. The engagement is broken off at the end of December.

The Mexican War ends.

1849 Poe is found only partly conscious and taken to a hospital on October 3. He dies on October 7 and is buried the next day with little ceremony.

TO FIND OUT MORE

BOOKS

Hayes, Kevin J. (editor), *The Cambridge Companion to Edgar Allan Poe.* New York: Cambridge University Press, 2002.

Quinn, Arthur Hobson. *Edgar Allan Poe: A Critical Biography.* Baltimore: Johns Hopkins University Press, 1998.

Silverman, Kenneth. *Edgar A. Poe: Mournful and Never-Ending Remembrance.* New York: HarperCollins, 1991.

Sova, Dawn B. *Edgar Allan Poe A to Z.* New York: Checkmark Books, 2001.

ORGANIZATIONS AND ONLINE SITES

Academy of American Poets
http://www.poets.org/poets/poets.cfm?prmID=131

This site includes a detailed biography, his poetry, and critical essays about his work.

All Poe
http://www.allpoe.com

This is eNotes' extensive Poe site. It has a good collection of critical articles on Poe's work.

The Baltimore Poe House and Museum
203 Amity Street
West Baltimore, MD 21223-2501
http://www.eapoe.org/balt/poehse.htm

The Baltimore Poe House and Museum is one of the places Poe lived in Baltimore. You can visit the house and see some items Poe owned and used. It is open from April to December.

Edgar Allan Poe National Historic Site
532 N. 7th Street
Philadelphia, PA 19123
http://www.nps.gov/edal/index1.html

In Philadelphia, the National Park Service runs Poe's Spring Garden house as the national memorial to Poe. He lived there from 1843 to 1844. You can visit it year-round.

The Edgar Allan Poe Society of Baltimore
http://www.eapoe.org/index.htm

This is the Web site of the Edgar Allan Poe Society of Baltimore, which contains a huge amount of interesting information.

Knowing Poe
http://knowingpoe.thinkport.org/default_flash.asp

This is Maryland Public Television's Knowing Poe site.

Letters of Edgar Allan Poe
http://etext.lib.virginia.edu/rbs/99/rbspoe99.html

Many of Edgar Allan Poe's letters are posted on this University of Virginia Web site.

Poe Cottage
The Bronx County Historical Society
Research Library and Administrative Headquarters
3309 Bainbridge Avenue
Bronx, NY 10467
http://www.bronxhistoricalsociety.org/index17.html

The Fordham, New York, cottage where Poe lived from 1846 to 1849 is now run by The Bronx County Historical Society. It looks like it did when Poe lived there. A film and guided tour are offered.

The Poe Museum
1914-16 E. Main Street
Richmond, VA 23223
http://www.poemuseum.org

The Poe Museum in Richmond, Virginia, is near Poe's first home in Richmond and the *Southern Literary Messenger* offices. It tells about Poe's time in Richmond. It also tells about his life and works in general.

Precisely Poe
http://www.poedecoder.com/PreciselyPoe/

The author of this site is an English teacher who is trying to solve the mysteries about Poe's life. You can ask questions about Poe controversies on the site.

University of Virginia
Guide Service
Pavilion 8 Lawn
Charlottesville, VA 22904
http://www.virginia.edu
http://scs.student.virginia.edu/~ravens/poe-rm.php

The University of Virginia has reconstructed Poe's dorm room on the West Range, behind the Lawn. It is set up as it would have been when he was a student there. There is a glass door so you can see in. You can visit it year-round.

A Note on Sources

Starting during his lifetime, people have written all sorts of biographies of Edgar Allan Poe. There have been many rumors and lies as well as truths told about him. His life story was interesting, confusing, and often sad. He got into mysterious messes and wrote wild letters. Some of the books about him try to analyze his story, some tell all the facts that can be documented, and some pass along the lies and exaggerations. This means it can be fun to read about him but hard to find the truth. The best books for sticking to the documented truth are Arthur Hobson Quinn's *Edgar Allan Poe: A Critical Biography* and Thomas Dwight's *The Poe Log.*

One of the best ways to learn about a person is to read what he and his friends have written themselves. Many of the letters Poe wrote and received are collected by the Library of Congress, the Enoch Pratt Free Library in Baltimore, and the Valentine Museum in Richmond. Some are available online, such as the University of Virginia collection. This is a good place to start. You can find it at *http://etext.lib.virginia.edu/rbs/99/rbspoe99.html.*

Some biographers look to Poe's poems and stories to explain what he really thought and felt. It is always hard to know how much an author bases his characters on his own personality or experiences. However much you learn about Poe's thoughts by reading his work, you can't help but understand why he is thought to be such a genius with words. There are many good collections of Poe's writings for you to read for yourself. I enjoyed rereading his poems and stories as I wrote this book. He was certainly a master at creating a mood and spinning a web in which to catch you up.

—*Tristan Boyer Binns*

INDEX

ABOUT THE AUTHOR

Tristan Boyer Binns has an English degree from Tufts University. She has written thirty books for children and young adults on subjects from the American flag to hermit crabs to saving energy. She has taught creative writing to children and adults and has run writing workshops. Before beginning her writing career, Tristan was publishing director for an international library book publisher. Researching people's lives and the history of daily life is a real joy for her.